A KWAKIUTL VILLAGE
AND SCHOOL

HARRY F. WOLCOTT
University of Oregon

WAVELAND
PRESS, INC.
Prospect Heights, Illinois

For information about this book, write or call:

Waveland Press, Inc.
P.O. Box 400
Prospect Heights, Illinois 60070
(312) 634-0081

In all people I see myself, none more and not one

   a barley-corn less,

And the good or bad I say of myself I say of them.

Walt Whitman, *Song of Myself*

ALERT BAY AND VICINITY, BRITISH COLUMBIA, CANADA

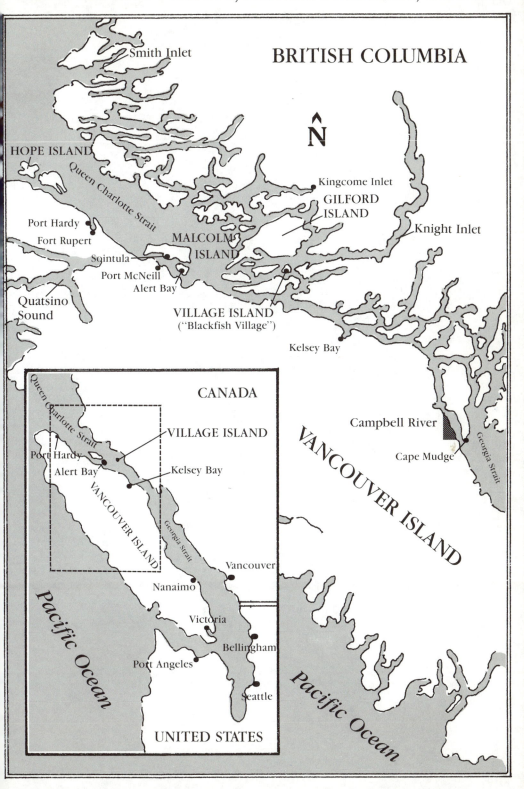

Foreword

About the Author

Harry F. Wolcott was born in Oakland, California in 1929. He took his undergraduate degree at UC Berkeley, graduating in 1951. Following military service, he turned to a career in education, studying for a master's degree at San Francisco State College while teaching public school in two California communities.

Awarded a Fellowship at Stanford University to pursue doctoral studies, he coupled cultural anthropology to his work as an educator with a formal Ph.D. minor in anthropology that included fieldwork among the Kwakiutl Indians of British Columbia, Canada. That research was first reported in a doctoral dissertation completed at Stanford in 1964, "A Kwakiutl Village and Its School: Cultural Barriers to Classroom Performance." At the invitation of George and Louise Spindler, the dissertation was rewritten for publication in the set of monographs with which the Spindlers launched the Case Studies in Education and Culture in 1967. For the most part, the study has remained in print ever since, most recently as reissued by Waveland Press.

After completing the dissertation, Wolcott accepted a research and teaching position at the University of Oregon, where he has held an appointment as Professor of Education and Anthropology since 1971. His major works include a study conducted in Zimbabwe, *The African Beer Gardens of Bulawayo* (Rutgers Center of Alcohol Studies), and anthropological studies of American education, including *Teachers Versus Technocrats* (University of Oregon) and *The Man in the Principal's Office: An Ethnography,* the latter monograph another of the Case Studies in Education and Culture reissued by Waveland Press.

Professor Wolcott has been a visiting lecturer/scholar in education and anthropology at the Universities of Alaska, Arizona State, McGill, and Northern Arizona, as well as a Fulbright Scholar at Kasetsart University, Bangkok, and a Research Associate at Universiti Malaya, Kuala Lumpur. He has been active in the Council on Anthropology and Education since its inception, having served terms as President and as Editor of its journal, the *Anthropology and Education Quarterly.* He is a member of the American Educational Research Association and a Fellow of both the American Anthropological Association and the Society for Applied Anthropology.

About the Book

This is an ethnography, selective in its focus and rich in its depth, of a contemporary North American Indian village on a small island and its school. A small group of Kwakiutl Indians, whose grandparents shared the aboriginal culture of the Northwest Coast in its most spectacular form, are the subjects of the case study. The ethnographer here is the teacher, and it is his school that he is describing.

The study is unique in its detailed description of the social environment from which the school draws its pupils and the interaction of these pupils with the teacher and the learning tasks set by him and the curriculum. By virtue of their separate origins the school and the village are separate entities, yet the intimate dependency of the educational activity upon the environment the village provides is apparent. The picture that emerges is at once tragic and hopeful. The frustrations issuing from miscommunications inherent in cultural differences are numerous and intense. Even more dramatic are those failures that issue from cultural disintegration. This Kwakiutl village has lost its coherent traditional culture, though many of its parts remain in force and, for reasons that become clear as this case study proceeds, has not acquired an integrated version of Canadian-American culture. The teacher and his school cannot reverse the process of disintegration; nevertheless, the people see education as the way to improve the lot of their children.

Though unique in many ways, Blackfish Village and its school are representative of schools and their environments everywhere. The school reflects its social environment, is a part of it, and yet is separate and accountable to forces and goals transcending the immediate community. The teacher is respected, sometimes loved, but also feared and sometimes hated. The pupils are distracted, disinterested, eager to learn, critical, and accepting. The divergent origins and orientations of pupils and their families versus those of the teacher and the school on Blackfish Island assign this case study general relevance for understanding the many other places in our modern world where technologically underdeveloped societies are using and being helped to use education as a vehicle for change. But the most direct and telling significance of this case study is for those many places in the world, including our own society, where teachers and schools are attempting to cope with the results in the classroom of social disorganization, cultural decay, linguistic inadequacy, and economic disadvantage. Perhaps the most important inference to be drawn from this study is that schools, teachers, teaching methods, and curriculum must adapt to reality as presented by the social environment in which they exist and that they cannot be held responsible for singlehandedly altering that environment. The problems and the frustrations inherent in them are legion, but one of the most significant steps is to try to understand them.

George and Louise Spindler

Stanford
1966

Preface

This case study is about a tiny Indian village along the inland waterway of the British Columbia coast. In a sense there are really two studies here, one of village life and one of the village school. While some of the principal actors— the village children of school age—are the same, the study illustrates a situation in which two educational systems, one essentially informal, indigenous, and present-oriented, the other essentially formal, external, and future-oriented, confront the children, their parents, and the appointed teacher with antithetical goals and a great range of real and potential conflicts. The teacher represents a formal educational system whose mission is to minimize traditional Indian culture. His official efforts in this direction are met by a variety of individual responses. The variations reflect the differences in the degree to which individual parents and children accept the ways of the dominant society that differ from traditional ways of the village.

The people and the situation represented in these pages are unique and yet highly representative. I have reported on a particular village, on particular children and adults, and on the particular course of events in the village during a year of field study when I was the teacher at the village school. A comparable study of even the closest neighboring village would reveal the kinds of differences that give each village and each school a personality in some ways unique. Still, those who have taught or observed in schools with other Indian children, or among children in certain sections of the big cities of North America, or among children in other parts of the world where a Western-oriented curriculum is being introduced under conditions of cultural stress, will recognize similarities in the behavior of pupils, parents, and teachers to those reported here.

For some eighty years anthropologists have been gathering data on the traditional and changing ways of life of the native peoples of the Northwest Coast. In the annals of anthropology the people of the village and of the immediate region are known as the Kwakiutl Indians. Franz Boas, sometimes referred to as "the father of American anthropology," continued to study and write about the Kwakiutl throughout his professional life. He is still remembered by many older natives. Ruth Benedict drew the chapter on the Northwest Coast of America in her *Patterns of Culture* from the Boas accounts. Many Americans carry about some image of the Kwakiutl Indians and of their great potlatches from reading her book. More recently Helen Codere has described major changes in Kwakiutl culture. Some references are included for those who wish to read further in the literature about either the Kwakiutl people or about Indian education in North America.

The study is presented in two major parts. Part One deals with village life and the social environment in which village children learn to become village adults. Villagers are neither isolated from nor oblivious to modern Canadian life. They listen to transistor radios, buy store clothes, purchase liquor at the government liquor store, collect unemployment benefits, and occasionally charter airplanes. At the same time they "hunt and gather" to make a wide use of many local food sources, they participate in Indian dances, and they "talk Indian." They return from their encounters with modern Canadian society to their own way of life in the village, a way that if not recognizably traditional, nonetheless has many links with the past. This is the culture of home, family, and village which surrounds the children. The children experience directly the skills, beliefs, and attitudes they would need if village life were never to change. Part One describes this way of life—what village adults and children do and how they talk and feel about what they do.

Part Two deals with a special and separate educational system operating within the village, one that is formal, directive, and highly focused. The purpose of the formal system is to "improve" the children and to provide them with personal resources so they can cope with a world in which skills of literacy and middle-class respectability have greater currency than knowing how to render eulachon grease or how to perform the dance of the *hamatsa* "cannibal dancer." Teachers, the village school and pupils, the classroom program, and attitudes toward formal education are described in Part Two. The problems which face the educator or the villager are too complex to warrant simple solutions, and no attempt is made to offer answers in this study. The reader is invited to ponder the problems as they emerge from the primary data presented.

The case study begins with an introduction which contains a description of the village and of the region. The introduction also includes a discussion about gathering the data.

I have attempted to write this account in the ethnographic present. However, many of the situations and events reported occurred only at one point in time, and there have been important changes in village life since 1962, the year of the initial study. Both of these factors make a consistent use of the present tense seem misleading. Thus I forewarn the reader that I have used both present and past tenses here, primarily with the intent of differentiating between recurring and unique events.

Although pseudonyms have been used for both village and villagers, the people and accounts given here are quite real. Ethnographers work for months or years among a group of people to try to record and understand every patterned kind of behavior and interaction. They then must decide what can and cannot be told to an audience whose motives are unknown and for whom there will never be an opportunity to make a full explanation. What is reported here is illustration, not indictment. The purpose is to make the villagers come alive as real and feeling human beings confronted at almost every step by a dominant society bent on changing the only way of life they know and persistently transmit.

H.F.W.

Eugene, Oregon
November 1966

Contents

Foreword   v

Preface   vii

Introduction   1

PART ONE—THE VILLAGE AND ITS CHILDREN   9

1. Features of Everyday Life   10

Dress and Appearance — Housing — The Families — Subsistence Activities and Diet — Health and Safety — Home Life — Children's Activities

2. The Annual Economic Cycle   32

Clam Digging — Springtime Activities — Logging — Villagers as Loggers — Fishing — Villagers as Fishermen — Augmenting Resources — Government Subsidy

3. Social Activities of Villagers   54

Formal Social Gatherings — Drinking — Sports Events — Travel — Religious Activities — Band Activities — Social Control

PART TWO—THE VILLAGE SCHOOL   67

4. The Educational Setting   68

The Residential School at Alert Bay — History of Formal Education at Blackfish Village — Indian Education within the Agency — The Blackfish Indian Day School

5. Parents and Teachers   78

   *The Educational Achievement of Village Adults — Attitudes
   toward Education — What Villagers Expect of a Teacher —
   Communication between Parents and the Teacher — The Behavior
   and Perceptions of Teachers*

6. The Pupils and the Classroom   95

   *Pupil Attitudes toward School and Teacher — The Classroom in
   Motion — Measures of Classroom Performance — Village Children as Pupils: Some Case Studies — Epilogue*

7. In Retrospect and Prospect   126

   *A Functional Assessment of Educational Needs — Cultural Values
   in the Cross-Cultural Classroom*

References   132

Afterword, 1989   133

Introduction

BLACKFISH VILLAGE is a very small village. At the time of my first visit, there were thirteen occupied houses and five vacant ones. Except for the large two-classroom schoolhouse and teacherage which stands above and separate from the rest of the village, the village today consists of only the frame houses plus an assortment of auxiliary buildings used for outdoor privies, smokehouses, and woodsheds. Traces of a church and other buildings that once stood in the community are fast disappearing. Only two totem poles and the house poles from two of the traditional "big houses" (multiple-family dwellings) give any specific clue that the local inhabitants are Indian.

Blackfish Island is also small, approximately six miles long and two miles wide. Of this area only 400 acres on the western shore of the island belong to the reserve. The village is hemmed in on the island side by a dense growth of berry vines and underbrush, and along the water's edge by a shallow, rocky shore which in low tides defies direct access. Around a point at one end of the village there is a protected harbor where villagers and visitors usually tie their boats. From the wharf and floats at this harbor, referred to by villagers as "the other side," a footpath known as "the road" extends up over a rise past the schoolhouse and on down through the village. The road is well graveled as far as the schoolhouse, after which it diminishes gradually to the width of a narrow trail which stops abruptly at an old totem pole at the far end of the village. The road parallels the beach. Two houses mounted on pilings that rise just above the high-water level stand between the road and the water's edge. The bank drops off steeply from the road to a narrow beach below.

In spite of the small physical size of the village and the fact that at most only fourteen households were ever occupied, this study deals with 125 Indian adults and children for whom, during the year of fieldwork, the village was home. The median age of the villagers was sixteen. "Seems like all there is is kids over there," was the way several people in the area described the village. As many as twenty-nine pupils were enrolled in the school at any one time during the year. The number of children and adults actually present in the village at any given moment was subject to great variation. While family and village ties are strong, they do not preclude a fairly easy movement of children and young adults among households and even from one village to the next.

The seeming ease with which at least some villagers make temporary changes of residence serves as a caution to describing the village as though its boundaries re-strict or delimit the world of the villagers. Anthropologists are not agreed whether the present-day villages adequately represent the boundaries of complete social groups or whether one must examine the social interaction of the people in *groups of villages* to describe the social system. The problem of defining social boundaries is further complicated by an attempt to determine how small a group can become and still maintain enough functions of social life to be considered a village. Blackfish Village is in some ways only a partial community, dependent upon and intricately linked with similar villages and with the town of Alert Bay. Still, the

Aerial view of Blackfish Village. (Courtesy of R. P. Rohner.)

village faces community problems, its permanent inhabitants are officially recog-nized through provisions of the Indian Act as a band unit, and its geographical iso-lation demands some sense of community among its inhabitants. I have not at-tempted to distinguish the degree to which it is appropriate to identify the village as a community in its own right and the degree to which the village is a partial or truncated community.

To most White Canadians, Blackfish Village is "just another Indian village." Villagers themselves perceive a social network consisting primarily of their band and eleven other village bands, although the Kwakiutl have never thought of them-selves as a unified people or "nation" (Codere 1961:432). Neighboring bands range in size from one of only two households to a band of several hundred mem-bers. Travel, friendships, and marriages are essentially limited to one's own and to the closest neighboring bands.

THE REGION

The town of Alert Bay is the regional center of activity for both the Indian and the non-Indian population. Two closer points where villagers can go for fuel, food, beer, and mail are made up of a general store, tiny post office, and beer parlor. For most shopping and business purposes, and for most social activity as well, villagers make the two-hour boat trip to Alert Bay.

Alert Bay is situated on Cormorant Island along Johnstone Strait, about 180 miles north of Vancouver, British Columbia. Large freight and passenger liners pass continually in the deep but narrow channel between Cormorant Island and Vancouver Island directly to the west. Alert Bay is served by a ferry boat connecting with bus service at Kelsey Bay that provides daily transportation to Vancouver. The overnight trip directly from Alert Bay to Vancouver by steamer takes fifteen hours. By air the trip from Vancouver via Port Hardy can be made in two hours.

Alert Bay's population was around 1200 in 1962. The population is divided about equally between Indian and non-Indian residents. Most of the Indian residents live on the section of the island that is reserve land. However, the majority of the commercial establishments are located off the reserve land.

Alert Bay provides a wide range of facilities and services among its stores and cafés, a bank, a post office, several government offices, and a land and water detachment of the Royal Canadian Mounted Police (RCMP). Four major Canadian oil companies operate marine fueling stations, and there are two shipyards. Three fishing companies maintain seasonal offices. In addition to the government liquor store, beer parlors in the two small hotels also sell beer to take out. The community hospital has three resident doctors and seventy beds. There are several churches with resident ministers. Village youths pay particular attention to the film fare at the two movie theaters.

Alert Bay has two schools, one a large public elementary-high school which all Alert Bay children attend, the other a six-teacher day school operated by the Indian Affairs Branch for Indian children from outlying villages. When the day school is in session, these children live at St. Michael's, the Anglican children's residence.

The "Indian office" at Alert Bay serves as official headquarters for the Kwawkewlth Indian Agency. In 1962 there were 2500 Indian adults and children registered throughout the area of the agency. The head administrative officer of the agency resides in Alert Bay and has two assistants and an office staff there. Properly his title is superintendent of the Kwawkewlth Indian Agency, but reference is always made to him as "the Indian agent" or "the agent."

Alert Bay is a modern frontier town. Its stable population, both Indian and non-Indian, is primarily concerned with logging, fishing, and mining activities in the area and with the services these primary industries require. In addition to its permanent residents it attracts adventurers, transients, and missionaries. On some weekends the town is deluged by itinerant loggers and fishermen. Except for business contacts, the majority of both the permanent White and Indian populations keep to themselves. While all the non-Indian inhabitants of Alert Bay are potential acculturators and representatives of the dominant society, most of their social behavior occurs within their own group. The Indian population has very limited access to models of White behavior other than among the transients or among the residents who drink beer in the beer parlors.

While Alert Bay is the center of activity for the region, the travel and interaction of villagers is not limited to only that one place. Smaller White and Indian settlements dot the area. Most of the interaction between Blackfish villagers and other Indians is with members of the three closest neighboring villages and with members of the large Nimpkish Band at Alert Bay.

Travel outside the vast area of the inland waterways does not take Blackfish villagers much beyond the territory their forefathers traversed. Seasonal fishing draws some fishermen north as far as Rivers Inlet and Namu for the sockeye salmon run in June and July, and wives and children often accompany the men on this trip. Few villagers have been as far north as Prince Rupert. The mountains of the Coast Range block access to the interior of British Columbia, although villagers do travel the great inlets that penetrate the mountains. In former times their migration pattern included an annual trip to the head of the spectacular Knight Inlet for catching eulachon, or candlefish, a fish about the size of a sardine, and for preparing eulachon grease. Blackfish Village sits close to the mouth of the inlet, and it is possible to travel sixty miles into the mainland by boat. Although fewer people make grease today, villagers do travel up the inlet for salmon fishing and hunting, and the trip is still a popular one.

Distant travel is predominantly to the south. Campbell River and Nanaimo on Vancouver Island are the nearest large communities. The two southernmost Kwakiutl Bands are at Campbell River and nearby Cape Mudge. During the year several village families and individuals traveled to Campbell River, most often traveling by boat directly from the village. An Indian hospital at Nanaimo serves the native population along the entire coast.

Vancouver, still farther south, is the "big city." Most village adults and a few children have been there. Late August, during the annual Pacific National Exhibition, is a popular time for making such a visit. However, this interferes with the fishing season, and more families talk about going to the "PNE" and about a summer trip to Vancouver than actually get there. Some villagers have traveled "to the States" to pick hops and berries just across the border in Washington. People who have made the trip like to discuss "conditions" in the States, particularly the ease with which beer and wine are purchased.

A few individuals born at Blackfish Village are now permanent residents of Vancouver. To move as far away as Alert Bay does not sever one from the local way of life. However, to go to Vancouver to live seems to be accepted as a rejection of village life. No reference by a villager to those who had moved to Vancouver contained any more information than the statement, "They went to Vancouver." Their absence serves only as an example of people who have gone far away; they are not models of acculturated Indians because they are not even known to the young people of the village.

Over the past twenty-five years there has been a steady migration of villagers moving from Blackfish Village to take up permanent residence in Alert Bay. Among the villagers who remain at Blackfish almost every adult and child expressed the wish to me at some time that he could move to Alert Bay and never return to the village. The move to Alert Bay has put former villagers in closer contact with the Whites with whom they deal in their fishing and in securing government assistance. It has provided greater access to medical facilities, to schools, and to many of the conveniences that modern life affords.

There are many criticisms of life at the Bay—it is getting "too rough," drinking is a greater problem there, living expenses are higher, and it is too easy to get into trouble and be picked up by the police. Because people originally from several bands now live together there, many of the sanctions which once governed behavior in smaller and more intimate band groups are no longer appropriate or effective. Adults rely on the police to maintain community order and even to discipline their own children; at the same time they are critical of any actions taken. In spite of the drawbacks and apprehensions, the migration of people from the outlying villages has continued.

A problem for the village is the selective nature of the migration. In the local phrase the "more progressive" people have left the village. As one villager observed:

> All those people who used to live at the village—they practically *run* the Bay. And they all good men. If they still here, we have a good village. The *best* one.

On another occasion a young village mother pondered, "How can things change [improve] here? There is no one who is a model of good behavior for these kids."

GAINING ENTREE AND COLLECTING DATA

My first visit to the Alert Bay region was in April 1962. I had the good fortune to know the regional superintendent of Indian schools for British Columbia. He invited me on an inspection of the schools so that I could see some of the villages where I might make my study and where, in return, I would help him with his recruiting problem by serving as a teacher in one of the isolated village day schools. Religious preference had already narrowed the list of possible schools where I could teach, for by statute the Indian Act assures that only Roman Catholic teachers can be sent to teach in areas where that faith predominates, and only Protestant teachers can be sent to Protestant areas. As a non-Catholic, I could be placed in schools in the Kwakiutl area because that region is officially Anglican.

Our tour included a visit to Blackfish Village and the Blackfish Indian Day School. The comparatively new school and teacherage there, the small class size (only twelve pupils at the time of our visit) and small village, the absence of other Whites, and the relative isolation of the village made it seem an ideal place to learn about the way of life of one village and of the relationship of school and village. I accepted an assignment as the teacher effective the following August.

As a thirty-three-year-old bachelor ("Where's you Mom?" the children asked me at first), I thought I had an advantage in not having obligations to a family of my own that would limit the time I could spend among villagers. Working alone created certain problems, however. I had to spend considerable time on domestic chores. I was unable to share my problems or my perceptions with a co-worker, nor could I benefit by the reflections on home life and child rearing which village women might have shared with a female observer. Since villagers rarely engage in any activity alone, they apparently assumed that I was lonely, and I had as many as twenty adults and children visiting in an evening.

As an experienced elementary-school teacher, I expected no difficulty in meeting my teaching obligation. I had not anticipated that the teacher image among villagers would be so stereotyped and that most role relationships are ready-made for any new teacher regardless of his personality or actions. In spite of this disadvantage, accepting the role of teacher as the vantage point for making a village study has some definite advantages for the ethnographer. Any person residing among a group of people has to have some role, and the teacher *role* is widely known and accepted even if the role occupant himself is not. The teacher role gives the fieldworker legitimate areas of inquiry among parents, particularly regarding expectations and hopes they hold for their children and how they expect the school to help. The teacher has access to village life through what the children say, write, and do. The children's attempts to socialize their teacher to ways appropriate to village life can provide him with many insights he would not get as quickly from contacts with the generally more reticent adults. The teacher also gives something of himself in his official capacity, so that his requests for help or information take on the nature of reciprocal actions.

As the teacher and a resident of the village, I kept journal entries of conversations, personal reactions, complaints, requests, and travel. I attempted literally to record everything I could force into consciousness. I was fortunate that nearly everyone in the village was bilingual and could speak to me in English. I understand little of the native language, Kwakwala, and only rarely did anyone volunteer a translation when villagers spoke it. My interest in learning native terms and my lack of mastery of the language place me somewhere between those ethnographers who insist that one can never do an adequate description of a people unless he understands their language and those past teachers who have refused to acknowledge the persistence of a native language or have prohibited its use within their presence.

I never assigned any villager the role of informant. Therefore, it was rarely appropriate to make written notes during conversations. By recording notes as soon as possible after conversations I was able to record the essence of most conversations. I pieced together autobiographical sketches of a few of the more verbal adults from conversations recorded throughout the year. One woman wrote a long autobiographical statement for me while she was convalescing in the hospital. As medical dispenser for eight months, I received occasional notes from parents. I received some requests for assistance with government forms and letters.

When the children became accustomed to writing as a daily part of the classroom work, they wrote quite frankly, and some of them, especially the two oldest girls, shared thoughts and activities they never discussed directly. I was not fully aware during my year of how valuable a source of data the daily writing of the children would be. Although my activities as teacher prevented my participation in concomitant activities in the village, I found that the children often described these activities with insights which I would not have had even if I had been present.

Classroom data also include recorded personal observations, sociograms, results of individual and group tests, notes and attendance records left by village teachers in the past ten years, official correspondence and publications of the Indian Affairs Branch, and interviews and correspondence with present and former teachers in the local schools.

When school closed at the end of June 1963, I had an opportunity to go fishing with villagers as an auxiliary crew member on a seine boat. At that time I experienced a major change in my perception of village life. The summer experiences as a fisherman provided an entirely different kind of participant-observation. The opportunity to change roles and to extend the range of experiences contributed immeasurably to a more complete and positive picture of village life.

Following a year's absence that was filled with a rather unexpected amount of correspondence from both adults and former pupils, I returned to join the seine crew during the latter part of the summer of 1964 and to revisit the village. I returned again in August 1965, and stayed until the close of that fishing season. During these visits I was able to talk to both new and returning teachers at local schools, to follow the progress of my former pupils, and to extend and correct my perceptions of village life. The epilogue to Part Two recounts some of the changes since the initial fieldwork.

PART ONE | The Village and Its Children

Part One describes the context in which all of village life except for activities concerned with the school is transmitted to the young. Much of this description of the village is related through the lives of five children and their separate families. The children are Joseph, 15; Norma, 14; Dorothy, 13; Walter, 12; and Reggie, 6. Their households represent different stages along an imaginary continuum in acculturative status from a relatively traditional to relatively acculturated way of life. Acculturation refers here to to the processes of adaptation which occur as members of the Indian culture increasingly come to accept a life style more characteristic of the dominant White society.

These children and their families appear again in Part Two. However, this description is not a child's-eye view of village life. The account is primarily concerned with adult and family activities and with the ways children learn what they will need to know as village adults. No attempt has been made to define how various activities exert differing degrees of influence on the children or to rank activities in the order of their importance. Children are neither consciously excluded from nor necessarily included in most adult activities. While children are not allowed to go everywhere all the time, they are never categorically denied participation. Doors are occasionally, but not often, closed to them. Any event from a band meeting to a drinking party may be part of the firsthand experience of at least some children and of vicarious experience for others. Indeed, the older children, because they circulate constantly throughout the village, usually have the most complete information about what is going on, while adults are inclined to "mind their own business."

This description of the village is presented in three sections. The first section deals with everyday life in the village. The second section, "The Annual Economic Cycle," describes the participation of villagers in their dominant work activities. This section also includes a discussion of other economic resources available to villagers. The third section, "Social Activities of Villagers," focuses on some of the recurring social situations.

1 / Features of everyday life

DRESS AND APPEARANCE

I T IS POSSIBLE today to find a village boy carrying a bow and arrow, wearing a headband with a feather stuck in it, and stalking either "game" or other Indian boys dressed in similar fashion. On one occasion a fourteen-year-old boy appeared with a feathered headband and the decorative marks of a war party painted on his arms, legs, body, and face. The occasion was the Halloween masquerade—the marks of war paint had been made with lipstick, and under a simulated breechcloth was the added protection of a pair of boxer-style swim trunks. When many village boys dress in "Plains Indian" fashion, a game of Cowboys and Indians is once again underway. Village boys usually wear T shirts or sport shirts, jeans, socks, and oxfords or tennis shoes. A dress-up occasion such as a wedding finds most boys dressed in a clean pair of jeans, and if possible, a white dress shirt. Inexpensive cotton wash pants or dark jeans are worn by most older boys and men. Jackets and bright sweaters are popular among both girls and boys, and the cold rainy climate makes such a wrap functional as well as colorful. Rubber "gum boots" are a standard item of clothing and every person has a pair of boots or has access to a pair.

Girls and young women wear pedal pushers, jeans, store dresses, or sweaters and skirts. Between the mail-order catalogs and several stores in Alert Bay they have a wide choice of clothing items. Price is seldom the first consideration in choosing clothing, but since there is no occasion in the village when special clothes are required, selections are made almost exclusively from low and moderately-priced clothing. Older women select print dresses and dark cardigan sweaters for everyday wear.

Mothers dress their babies in store diapers, rubber pants, baby blankets, and in the pastel blues and yellows of infant dress typical in urban life. Bassinets and baby carriages are in evidence in many homes and are shared among relatives upon the arrival of a new baby.

Many mothers, particularly those with smaller families, take pleasure in dressing their young children in nice-looking clothes. However, a child has no extra restrictions placed on his activities when "dressed up," so fancy clothes usually have a short life. Among older children, especially the boys, new clothes are often worn continually from the time of purchase.

The skin color of the villagers ranges from quite light to rather dark. Adults

Village children.

whose complexions are light and who have passed as Whites may recount such tales with delight. Writing a pen-pal letter to a White girl, Norma said of herself, "My skin is tan because I go swimming a lot." Tan is a good description of the average skin color. Males tend to have light beards and consequently their faces are not made darker by beard shadows. A few men have rather serious cases of acne.

The adolescents seem self-conscious about their appearance. Some teenagers are acutely aware of skin blemishes, and at least one youth rubbed Noxzema on his chin hoping to prevent pimples. Teen-age girls and women exchange turns at washing and setting each other's hair and young women in the village often wear bandanas to cover plastic curlers. The boys seem to be constantly combing their long, dark hair, and a rat-tail comb sticks out of the rear pocket of nearly every youth. Many children have never been to a barber shop, since haircuts are generally given by parents. Baldness is practically unknown among the men and is considered to be a characteristic of the White man about which the children, at least, laugh openly.

The average height of Indian adults is less than that of the White population. Many of the older Indian people of the region, particularly the women, are rather obese, a consequence of a lack of self-consciousness about gaining weight, an inadequately balanced diet with an excess of carbohydrates, and, for the women, their many years of childbirth. Local doctors feel that most of the villagers' diets lack sufficient calcium and iron. This is a general problem in the region and a severe one for certain village families.

While the rate of dental decay may not differ appreciably between the Indian and non-Indian population, villagers make no provision for dental care. No dentist treated a villager during the year, although doctors pulled many teeth. Full dentures are common even among older teenagers. A well-established fad among teenagers, particularly the boys, is to have the upper incisors pulled out after convincing the doctor that these teeth "bother" them. This emphasizes a fang-like appearance of the upper cuspids and is highly characteristic of the adolescent boys and young men at Blackfish Village.

HOUSING

Village homes are all of light-frame construction. The dwellings are single-family units based on a simple floor plan of a front room, kitchen, one or possibly two bedrooms downstairs, and, in the larger houses, additional rooms upstairs. All village houses are raised off the ground, and in most cases the space under the house is used for storage. All houses have front steps and some kind of front porch. Most houses face the water. Every house can be boarded up and locked, but in its owner's absence it can as easily be unboarded and unlocked.

The village was the first among the outlying villages of the area to have electrical power, and for almost twenty-five years villagers operated their own diesel electric generator. A few years ago the last of several generators gave out, and there is little likelihood of obtaining another replacement. Power poles and remnants of power lines still stand in the village, and there are electric outlets in the houses.

Some houses or parts of houses show signs of recent painting—usually because the agent donated some paint or because there was some left over from painting a boat. The external appearance of a house and yard is usually a good indication of the care accorded the interior of the house. Dorothy's house boasts a picket fence, window boxes, and venetian blinds. Reggie's grandparents' house, where Reggie and his family stay, is a large two-story house that is as pleasantly cluttered and hospitable as a typical midwest farmhouse. At the other extreme are houses which contain little furniture and which are seldom swept or cleaned.

A few households have inside cold-water taps, although no completely dependable supply of water exists in the village. Several fresh-water taps stand along the village road. Water is pumped from the village well to a large storage tank on a hill above the school by means of a small gasoline-operated pump. Since the storage tank leaks and the children often turn on the taps and leave them running, the pump has to be run each day. The pump house is locked to protect the pump machinery and the well and to protect the fuel supply from villagers who would use it to operate boats or outboard motors. The primary responsibility for the operation of the pump was delegated by the chief councillor to an older man who was usually at the village. This man faced perpetual criticism for the undependable supply of water and for his sometimes undependable operation of the pump. Yet he was often unable to find an adult who would temporarily take charge of the key when he was going to be away. His position was made even more difficult by occasional demands for fuel for personal use. More than once the key was in Alert Bay (often in a beer parlor and once locked up in jail) while villagers went without running water.

Water shortages present problems in most outlying villages. The problem has become so severe at Blackfish that during some summers the women and children have had no alternative but to leave the village and join the men at fishing or move in with relatives in other communities.

In September 1962, there were fifteen houses that were habitable. Three other houses were relatively intact except for missing windows and doors. Vacant houses have a short life once the children begin to play in them. Adults and children alike often hasten the destruction by removing boards for use as fuel or for minor construction. A command to the children not to play in an old house and not to tear it apart might impede or even prevent such destruction, but the order never seems to come. Villagers are not inclined to interfere in the actions of others that do not directly concern them.

Two sets of house posts which stand in the village mark sites where two village big houses once stood. Within the memory of older villagers band members lived together in groups of families in these and similar multiple-family dwellings. Each nuclear family of husband, wife, and children residing in one of the big houses had its own cooking fire and sleeping quarters, while groups of families shared a large fire and area in the center of the house. The groups of families living together tended to be members of the same numimot,[1] the basic kinship and social group of traditional Kwakiutl social organization. The notion of numimots is carried about today only in the minds of a few old people. Younger people are unaware of these social units and have been raised entirely in single-family dwellings. Each household today consists of one nuclear family, although additional kinsmen usually reside in the house.

THE FAMILIES

The children on whom this account focuses all lived with their parents. Fifteen-year-old Joseph lived in one of the smallest houses with the biggest family in the village, a total of seven sisters, five brothers, two nieces, and his mother and father. Norma, the youngest daughter of a large family, lived with her widowed mother and an ever-changing household of siblings, nieces, and nephews. Dorothy and her younger brother, her only sibling, comprised one of the smallest families. Walter shared a house with his parents, two older sisters, a brother-in-law, and six other brothers. Little Reggie, during his stay in the village, lived with his grandparents at their house with his siblings, his parents, and other aunts and uncles. For the most part, the present male heads of households are sons of villagers and they have brought wives to the village to live. All wives except one have come from villages within the immediate region of other Kwakwala-speaking villages, for the shared-language boundary circumscribes the villages from which a villager will normally find a wife.

Sharing a common language provides the means by which natives of the region identify themselves as a group in contrast with more distant tribes. The only term

---

[1] The term numimot has been anglicized by Rohner to identify the Kwakwala term *nə mi'* *mot,* the Kwakiutl ambilateral corporate descent group (Rohner, 1967). See also Rohner-Bettauer, *The Kwakiutl: Indians of British Columbia* (1986 reissue) Waveland Press, Inc. Prospect Heights, IL.

by which the people refer to themselves collectively in their native language in any group larger than a band is by a term that means "Kwakwala-speaking." Kwakwala still predominates in the village today. It is spoken almost exclusively by the oldest women, including Norma's mother, and is used extensively by most adults and by those children who have lived all their lives in the village. The only household where Kwakwala is not spoken in adult conversation is the one in which the wife comes from a different region. Since her native language and that of her husband are mutually unintelligible, they have no alternative but to communicate in English. English is the first language of their children.

Village women generally go to the village of their husband to reside. Under provisions of the Indian Act a woman's official band membership changes to her husband's band at the time of marriage. Two young village women and their husbands described themselves as "temporary" residents in the village. For both couples the husband's village had diminished so in size that they never intended to return there, yet the couples did not consider themselves band members, and they did not take part in official band activities. The return of Reggie's parents to the village was regarded as temporary because Reggie's father is from a different band.

The Indian agent records official band memberships and band transfers. In addition to the official, formal transfers from band to band, there is an unofficial system of the "old" or "Indian way" of reckoning alignment which operates on the principle that in the social and traditional sense a man's band never changes regardless of where he resides. In the "Indian way" the band has never lost those members who moved to Alert Bay, and their social obligations, like their kin obligations, persist. Such ties may be valued more by villagers who have remained behind, but they are not ignored even by the people who have moved away.

Regardless of the strife that occurs within the family group, each village family presents a compact and united front to any threat—verbal, physical, or imagined— from another family group or from outsiders like the Indian agent, the RCMP, or the teacher. Within each family group the combined range of activities and resources provide a relatively stable and self-sufficient way of life. The activities of the members of any one household usually complement a larger group than the immediate household itself. For example, with so few boats available to provide transportation, villagers who lack this resource themselves usually have access to the boats of others by demands they can make through kin obligations.

SUBSISTENCE ACTIVITIES AND DIET

"In the old days we ate food, but now we eat money," a villager once observed. His remark was prompted as we passed an island where there had been a summer village at which the people formerly gathered to catch and dry halibut for their winter food supply. At this summer moment, by contrast, the villager was at the wheel of a purse seiner heading toward one of the commercial salmon fishing areas. The salmon to be caught in the next few days were not for eating but would be delivered to company packer boats, shipped to Vancouver, and canned for Canadian and world markets. Instead of a smokehouse full of barbecued salmon, the Indian fisherman works for a pocket full of cash—cash with which he can buy goods at the store.

Villagers have not entirely substituted "money-gathering" activities for food-gathering ones. The region is still rich in food resources. While a few village families are almost totally dependent on the cash economy, others are almost able to get by solely through subsistence activities. The subsistence-oriented family today may not have the abundance of natural resources once known to the area, but new sources augment traditional ones. Such new sources include welfare payments from the Indian agent, intermittent cash income, and the larder of more affluent villagers, especially one's relatives.

Students who have studied the availability of food resources in earlier Kwakiutl history receive conflicting firsthand reports from older informants and find in the literature various economic explanations for the social organization of the Kwakiutl, particularly as epitomized in the potlatch feasts.[2] Apparently there have been times of genuine famine, but between land and water resources there has always been some food available to the resourceful. On several occasions people said, "No Indian around here will ever starve." The intent of this statement may be variously interpreted. First, the area continues to provide an abundance of food resources. Second, the statement implies solidarity among the Indian people—they can count on each other when necessary. Third, the idea may be a reaction to the fact of the ultimate dependence of most Indian people today on the dominant economy. In one instance of extreme hardship during the year, villagers made no major effort to help a destitute family but complained instead, "What's the matter with the Indian agent, letting that family starve like that?"

Villagers who rely primarily on subsistence activities have considerable annual variation in their diet. Clams can be dug for domestic use for about eight months. Large crabs are easily taken from the beach in front of the village during periods of extremely low tides and in traps at other times. Other animals of the intertidal zone, such as abalone and barnacles, are collected at special times and places, especially in the spring. Seaweed is collected and dried in the spring for use as a vegetable. Bottom fish, particularly rock cod, ling cod, and red cod are easily caught by "jigging," fishing with a hook and lure. When a buyer is in the area, jigging becomes a source of ready cash as well as a source of food for table use and for smoking or drying. Halibut is a favorite for eating and for drying and storing and local halibut reach such size that occasionally one man fishing in a skiff cannot bring the fish into the boat. Salmon and eulachon are important to the diet of all villagers, but neither fish is generally sought today in a subsistence fashion. The most common means of getting salmon today is for the fisherman in the family to bring fish back to the village on his return from the week's commercial fishing. A few spring salmon are caught on lines.

During the fall and spring, ducks and geese fly over the village in great numbers; during the fall migration a shot may ring out at any time when the birds are in low flight. Smaller birds like pheasant are occasionally shot. Older people comment on having eaten sea gulls, but these birds are not eaten today.

---

[2] Traditional potlatch ceremonies were marked by the giving away or destroying of property.

Deer and berries are predominant in the food resources available from the land. A variety of wild berries grow immediately behind the village, and from spring to fall these vines provide food. Berries are put up in quantity as jams and preserves during the summer.

Deer are "in season" for subsistence hunting any time the game warden or police are not around, and these officials are not frequently present in the outlying villages. Indians may get special permits when they wish to hunt or fish exclusively for their own use, but villagers do not always bother with this formality. Deer hunting begins with a boat trip, and ideally the hunt is conducted completely from the water. The most popular method of bagging a deer is to shoot it on a cliff where it will roll down to the water's edge. Whenever boats travel near the shore the men and older boys scan the brush for deer. I have seen a seine crew abandon fishing for an hour so a crew member could chase a deer into the brush. Night hunting with a beam of light ("pit-lampin' ") is illegal but is practiced both out of need and for sport.

Occasionally, preparations are made by groups of men for a foray into the back country, via the inland waterways, in a large-scale hunting trip. Such trips are discussed enthusiastically and are made in the spirit of a holiday. The potential bag of such a hunt includes black bear and white mountain goats in addition to deer. Some men rely on their skills to provide food for their dependents, and sanctions against a hunter who violates a sportsman's standards are mild. Seeing a small young deer which one man had shot, another joked, "He better not let the game warden see him with that jack rabbit."

No family is completely independent of the White man's diet. Sugar, flour, canned milk, and tea are staple purchases for every household as finances and shopping trips permit. That combination of staples is so frequent a grocery order that storekeepers refer to it as "standard Indian." Beans, potatoes, rice, cereals, and macaroni are frequent purchases. The food preferences of a few families show the influence of shopping patterns similar to those of a middle-class housewife except that villagers buy little meat and then only the easily prepared and inexpensive cuts. Frankfurters and baloney are favorites.

Bread and butter or margarine are served with most meals. Villagers bake wonderful big loaves of bread, although they prefer store bread when it is available. Bread and soda crackers, perhaps enhanced with peanut butter or jelly, are popular snacks throughout the day for children of the more affluent families. Generously iced sheet cakes or sweet rolls are baked as special treats in most houses.

Tea or coffee is served with meals. Sugar and evaporated milk are used liberally by children and adults in tea and coffee. Children also enjoy punch drinks prepared from commercial syrup bases. No household has a working refrigerator or ice, so dairy products except for butter and cheese are never purchased. Powdered milk is used in cooking but is not prepared for drinking.

Vegetables, usually purchased in small amounts, are primarily of the root variety which keep well. Salads are seldom prepared; tomatoes, lettuce, or cabbage provide the ingredients when they are. Fruit is popular but is quite expensive because of shipping costs. A few old fruit trees grow in the village, but they are not cared for and the children usually pick the fruit before it is ripe.

The natural food resources of the area are included in the diet of every household. Villagers do not disparage the efforts of others in utilizing subsistence foods. One of the threatening problems that faces anyone who contemplates leaving the village is the realization that one cannot count on his ability to tap primary food resources if secondary economic sources fail. Reggie's mother explained the problem faced by her husband when they considered leaving the village for another try at urban life:

> When we go back, it's hard for him because he can't go out digging or fishing when there isn't work. You just can't go out and work that way, you have to keep a job.

When parents are away, children in some families have their meals with relatives, while children in other families are left to fend for themselves. Occasionally young children beg food and are given handouts at a kitchen door. Children who beg in this fashion are not trusted when they claim at other times that they have been sent to "get a loaf of bread for my dad."

I know of no instance of a formal dinner invitation, although if a welcome visitor happens to be in the house at mealtime or when coffee is about to be served, he is included without any invitation except for a comment such as, "It's ready." Regardless of what "it" is, the guest is expected to partake.

Children are not forced to eat foods they do not care for nor are they often coerced into eating. No concern or disappointment is expressed if a teenager or adult announces just before mealtime that he does not feel like eating. The daily schedule of the village school makes almost the only demand on mealtime regularity, and even then an endeavor to attend school punctually is sometimes compromised by a stove that will not light, beans that do not get cooked on time, or the clean-up chores after a meal expected of school-age children.

Walter once wrote to explain why he and his brother were late returning to school:

> I was washing dishes this after dinner with Raymond and I was packing woods to me and my brother and this is my best brother always helps me.

A return from a shopping trip or from a good day's hunting or fishing is often the occasion for a big meal. Here is Walter's brief description of a successful hunt:

> We went out hunting at 9:30 and we came back at 10:30 and we got one deer and we eat it up the afternoon. Gee it was taste good. Boy it was good. So good.

While their written comments in class occasionally described their most recent meal or some special food, if the children were at times genuinely hungry, they never recorded it. The following three excerpts from the writing of a twelve-year-old girl tell something of her diet for a week during the winter:

> My brother got seal Monday and I like to ask you Mr. Wolcott if you want some from the seal. There good to eat. We have some for supper time.

. . .

> My father got a deer this morning when he went hunting. Maybe we might have some for supper.

. . .

My father can the deer yesterday. We got no more seal. We finished it Sunday. We had it for supper and we had deer for dinner today.

Before their kitchen fires go out in the evening, villagers often have a final snack. In some homes this evening "mug-up" provides a fourth meal of the day. The mug-up in Reggie's grandfather's house occurs in the evening between nine and eleven o'clock. It consists of tea or coffee, bread or crackers, jam or peanut butter, and sometimes a treat like fruit cocktail or freshly baked rolls or cake. In that household the children are permitted their own little mug-up before retiring—their choice leans toward peanut butter and jelly.

The very numbers in some of the larger families preclude all members sitting down at the table together. When women and children are along on a seine boat the men usually eat first at a separate sitting. The same arrangement holds in some homes. Family size, facilities for eating, and formality about dining vary considerably, but there is some preference for all members of a household who are immediately available to eat together.

HEALTH AND SAFETY

Medical and religious services for the native population were usually offered concurrently in the past. The Anglican church continued to provide both kinds of service during the year, although subsequently its efforts have been limited to religious work. The Anglican church serves the village by means of the mission boat "Columbia." The boat always carried a doctor but only occasionally a clergyman. Although the calls of the Columbia were never announced in advance to villagers, the possibility of the boat's presence in the vicinity provided a potential source of medical help in emergencies.

The services of three doctors and a well-equipped local hospital are available in Alert Bay, only minutes away from the village by airplane. During my stay in the village, several people were flown to Alert Bay for emergency medical attention. Even at night the trip can be made by boat in two hours except in the very worst weather.

The Indian office pays the expense for most medical service to Indian people, and villagers make extensive use of these free services. More than half of the villagers either were patients at the hospital at Alert Bay or were treated by doctors there during the year. Because of the image they hold of the care of the sick in Indian homes, hospital personnel are inclined to accept patients, particularly infants, when there is any suspicion of a serious illness, and they do not release patients until recovery is almost complete. Such a practice is quite acceptable to Indian parents who are glad to be relieved of the responsibility of a sick child. Indian parents become annoyed if a child is not accepted as a patient.

Indian people are considered by hospital staff to be passive and "good" patients, generally uncurious about their treatment or prognosis. By hospital custom male Indian patients share wards with Whites but the women are separated. One exception to the "good patient" stereotype is the older Indian women, whom nurses report as being quite demanding of care and attention, similar to the demands they can make on daughters and daughters-in-law in their own homes.

Although the Kwakiutl as a group have been described as pragmatic about drawing on the resources of medical technology, neither modern medical practices nor local doctors receive their unqualified endorsement. Reggie's father reported that a doctor once told his wife that the baby she was carrying was dead inside her. He instructed the doctor not to give his wife pills or injections of any kind, and he told him, "Your medicine is no good." His wife had a normal delivery.

Many people state a preference for the treatment at the Nanaimo Indian Hospital. This hospital formerly specialized in the treatment of tuberculosis but today accepts Indian patients for a variety of long-term treatments. Seven persons from Blackfish Village spent extended periods of time at this institution during 1962–1963. Once a year staff members from the Nanaimo Indian Hospital make a regional tour by boat of all villages, offering x-rays to all adults and children, and medical examinations to school-age children. With coaxing, the villagers' response to the x-ray opportunity was good but not 100 percent. No new cases of tuberculosis were reported. The doctor was delighted to see that his previous recommendations of tonsillectomies for several children had been carried out at the local hospital.

Additional medical service is provided by the Indian Health Service of the Department of National Health and Welfare. Two nurses from the Indian Health Service maintain a clinic at Alert Bay and hold one-day clinics each month in the outlying villages. After all the school children are checked, one of the nurses makes home visits while the other sees infants and adults who come to the school where the clinic is set up in the unused classroom. Although I never heard of a child who was afraid to go to the hospital, village children were resentful of the nurses' arrival because their visits inevitably meant "pokes" (injections). The fear of the pokes is widespread; some Indian youngsters become apprehensive at the sound of an airplane and cry at the sight of any non-Indian stranger in the village. I heard an Indian father explain to White visitors why his daughter wailed so in their presence: "She thought you were nurses." Literally every daytime visit of infants to the village school is for a "poke" administered by a non-Indian.

Families differ considerably in their acceptance of the nurses as friends and advisors. Some families attempt to avoid the nurses or refuse to come to the door when the nurse visits. The nurses endeavored all year to enlist the cooperation of one family in treating the children's scalp for head lice. The nurses shampooed the children's hair and then requested the reluctant mother and oldest sister to cut the children's hair and to continue the treatment. "We're Indians, and we think different about these things than you," the sister replied. Yet in some households the visit of the nurses is welcome and their advice and approval are eagerly sought.

The Indian Health Service attempts to provide a dispensary at each village where first-aid supplies, vitamins, Lysol, cough medicine and similar items are available. Often this task falls to the teacher's family and adds a modest increment ($20 per month at Blackfish Village) to his income. Villagers who utilized this free service drew most heavily on the aspirin supply and the locally popular "Two-twenty-two's" (aspirin-phenacetin-codeine). Such requests typically followed a night of partying.

Village life is not conducive to systematic pill-taking in most households. When a person does take pills there is a tendency to take an overdose and to expect fast results. Dorothy wrote this description of how she "cured" a cold:

> On Monday night I took a hand full of "222." I don't know how many there was though. On Tuesday I sweat it out all day. That is why I never came to school.

I heard of no instance of the present-day use of native curers, and the only reference to native medicines were references to the healing qualities of eulachon grease. The grease is normally eaten as food, but a person who is ill may take an extra quantity as medicine and may rub grease on his chest or back. It is believed that the grease keeps one in good health when included as a regular part of the diet. "Make good stomachs and no get sick," explained one father as five of his young children sat in a circle around a bowl of grease dipping shoots of Indian rhubarb into it and eating them in a little impromptu picnic.

Medical surveys support the firsthand observation that the accident rate among the native population is high. A study made in one recent year (Schmitt and Barclay 1962) revealed that the number of deaths was greater among the Indian than the non-Indian population throughout British Columbia for *every major cause* of accidental death. Drowning is the most frequent cause of accidental deaths; ten times more Indians than non-Indians died from drowning in that year. The Indian population, comprising just over 2 percent of the total population of British Columbia, accounted for almost 20 percent of the deaths due to drowning in the province.

The year was a particularly tragic one for the tiny village population in terms of accidental deaths. In two separate accidents, eight villagers, including three children and one teenager, lost their lives by drowning. A ninth accidental death occurred to a child living away from the village; the only nonaccidental death was that of an infant who was under hospital treatment at the time. Drinking was involved in both drowning accidents, although the extent of drinking will never be known in either case. Drinking is often a factor in accidents either directly or indirectly through the neglect of children once the partying starts.

Another factor contributing to accidents is the native tendency to act impulsively, without regard for long-range consequences. Fishing and logging put men in situations where equipment often becomes jammed. Among the ways to get things operating again there is usually one alternative which requires an element of chance or personal danger. In such a case, an Indian man, particularly a younger one, may step in to assume the risk. If you were to ask a man who took such a risk if he was concerned about getting hurt, he would be likely to reply, "I just didn't think about that." In a similar context I once asked in adolescent boy if he was apprehensive when he found himself in a fight. He replied that he "never gives it a thought." Then he added, "That's the trouble with you White guys, you always worry about what's going to happen."

Boat safety is not ignored but few boats carry all the safety equipment required by law. The local solution to carrying too few life preservers is to keep a sharp lookout for the RCMP Marine Patrol and to hide extra riders from the patrol. Before a gill-net boat left the village for Alert Bay one day the skipper realized that he had seventeen passengers on this thirty-foot boat. A villager does not expect to be refused a ride.

HOME LIFE

A village woman fulfills herself by caring for her husband and by raising children. Reflecting on bringing up her large family, Reggie's grandmother said, "Oh, I'm so happy with all my children." Indian parents hold no notion of an ideal family size. There is no goal to "have" a family in the sense that parents some day decide not to have more children. Nor do parents anticipate a day when their children will all grow up and leave the household. When she is too old to have children of her own, a village woman will have grandchildren in her home to care for, or she may take the responsibility for bringing up someone else's children. No village household had fewer than two children. The oldest couple in the village had two school-age grandsons living with them whom they were rearing as their own children. The boys were so used to living with their grandparents that they addressed them as father and mother and called their own parents by different kin terms. The immediate world of every village child includes relations of all ages from siblings near his own age to parents, grandparents, and sometimes great-grandparents. In his daily activity no child's associations are ever limited solely to other siblings and young parents.

Family sizes ranged from one recently married couple without children (although there had already been two miscarriages) to a family of, to use the mother's phrase, "thirteen *living* children." Even in such a large family it was her lack of care of the children rather than the size of the family that caused comment among other villagers. In speaking about the mother, one woman said in a slightly disapproving tone, ". . . and I think she's carrying [pregnant] again." She was.

Mothers usually carry their smallest children with them when visiting or when travelling from the village. Once a child is able to walk about on his own he is less likely to accompany his parents and more apt to be left in the care of an older sibling. By that age, his mother's attention is probably focused on a newborn. Infant care is not the exclusive domain of the mother; babies are fed and held by any nearby adult or older child. Feeding is on demand, and a crying infant generally receives immediate attention. Village women bottle-feed their children from birth. Some young mothers express the wish that nursing would be accepted by the women, but no woman wishes individually to oppose the existing custom. The standard bottle formula consists of a mixture of canned milk and hot water from a kettle. One of Walter's entries illustrates the casual nature of caring for a baby:

> We got up at 6:00 o'clock this morning so I put the stove on and it was hot so I put some milk in the bottle so I give it to the baby.

The men accept their large families without reflecting about them too much. Reggie's father stated that he would like to have "a dozen" children, but he added that because his wife had trouble with her fourth child he was "cut off" at the time. In spite of his lament, nine months later he had another son.

The husband's role strikes a balance between time spent with his wife and family and his pursuit of a variety of activities through which he can escape from both family and village. When they are home, the men may look after the children, do the cooking, or help in other housework. Some men are said to be better cooks than their wives, and village boys boast of their competence in preparing meals.

Husbands with dominating wives find ways to escape their directives. Staying away from the house or village is one way. Drinking, either at home or as an alternative to returning there, provides a route of escape from household routine for men and for some wives as well. The following vignette illustrates how a husband took exception to his wife's directives, and how he coped with them. The husband had stayed at the village to care for the children while his wife was in the hospital for the birth of another child. Several people hopped a ride to Alert Bay with the husband when he went to pick up his wife and child, and some of them brought beer when they returned to the village with him. After depositing his wife and four-day-old baby at his home, the husband went to have a few beers at another house. Twice his wife sent their oldest daughter to tell the husband to come home, but he sent the child away with the message that he would return soon. Finally his wife appeared in person, pale and shaking. "Are you crazy?" she asked him. "Sitting here getting drunk all the time. You should come help me. I should be in bed. The children are running all around."

"They weren't running around when I was there."

"You should be helping me instead of getting drunk."

"I can't get drunk on two cases of beer."

"You should come help me," she repeated, and she went to the door to leave.

"I'll be down in a minute," he added.

"Aw, bull shit," she yelled, and she slammed the door closed and returned home.

"If she's going to be that way, I think I'll just stay drunk for awhile like I did *last* year when the baby was born," he commented. At that time he said he had stayed drunk for two weeks.

According to a local doctor, most native women do not use contraceptives in spite of the physical demands of their large families and their frequent pregnancies. A doctor at the Indian hospital had urged one village mother, age thirty, to take oral contraceptive pills. She had recently given birth to her eighth child and was badly crippled with arthritis which made housework exhausting for her. She took the pills primarily because of her respect for the doctor. She expressed anxiety over recent publicity that led her to believe that she was taking a pill which had caused the death of many women and which might be very dangerous to her. Because of similar fears and misapprehension regarding the use of oral contraceptives, plus the reluctance on the part of doctors to give unsolicited advice on birth control, little recent change has been effected in the traditional practice of having large families.

Differences in housekeeping practices and general cleanliness among families are remarkable. In two households little attention was paid to cleanliness. Children from these houses often wore the same clothes day and night for many days at a time. Cheeks and arms of the very young children in both houses were chapped, arms and legs had scratches and cuts that had become infected, the children had scabs from constantly dripping noses, and they had hair lice. By contrast, children from most village homes are quite clean; they live in clean houses and wear clean clothes in spite of the problems their parents encounter keeping them that way. Dirt and mud are never farther than a few steps from the kitchen or front door and are tracked through the houses by the constant traffic of adults and children. Toiletting, replenishing the wood supply, "spilling the pots," dumping garbage, and, in most homes, obtaining water, require trips out of the house. Still, floors are generally clean and linoleum rugs are scrubbed and polished. In some households the effort at cleanliness can be described as compulsive. At our first meeting one village mother expressed her dissatisfaction with village life because it is so difficult to keep children, clothes, or house clean, particularly with the chronic water shortage. "I just hate a dirty place," she commented. "I really like to keep my kids clean, especially their pajamas and all."

Beside the routine functions of washing, cleaning, and cooking, the women do varying amounts of baking, preserving, canning, and sewing. On occasion all the adults of a household or family group cooperate in a large-scale operation such as putting up clams or berries for family use. Deer is cooked and put up as deer stew (the term venison is not used locally). When village men do their "own-use" fishing for salmon the entire adult population of the village is likely to be engaged in barbecuing or smoking and canning the fish for several days.

The different ways men in the village approach their task of providing the household with wood reflect the range of attitudes toward preparing for the future, toward where and how one uses resources, and toward one's self-sufficiency. I heard a man in one village complain bitterly that he should be paid by the Indian agent for the time he spent chopping wood for his parents.

Like many subsistence activities, obtaining logs initially involves a boat trip and can sometimes be done completely by boat. Logs that have washed up on the beaches are the source of supply. During their boat travels the men watch constantly for and make mental note of the location of good logs.

"In the old days we used to get wood for all the people. Everyone helped and in a day or two we had enough wood for two to three months. Now when you walk down the road people don't even speak to you." This comment was voiced by Reggie's grandfather, who must either provide logs for several other families or risk having his cut wood stolen from his woodshed. Four households in his own family are directly dependent on him for wood. With his large seine boat and with the help of his sons and sons-in-law, he can find and tow many logs to the village at one time, and there is always a supply of logs tied up on the beach in front of his house. By giving logs to his less fortunate neighbors, Reggie's grandfather hopes they will at least cut and carry their own wood. This is the only way that he can "get ahead" on his own wood supply.

Joseph's father, Joseph's older brothers, and occasionally Joseph himself cut up logs given to them by Reggie's grandfather. When the men of that family are not available to cut the logs, the younger children knock boards from a vacant house or steal wood from available woodpiles. At one point during the winter Joseph's father and oldest brother and several other village men were serving short jail sentences, and most wood supplies were exhausted. Joseph and another teen-ager spent most of a day cutting up logs on the hill behind the school. All the younger children in the two households assisted in carrying blocks of wood down to the houses. Adequate as it was, this was not the usual way of getting firewood among villagers, and in response to my "How's it going?" Joseph felt the need to explain, "We've got no boat."

The men sometimes pick berries, make minor engine adjustments to their boats, mend and repair equipment, or look after the children so that their wives can hop a ride to Alert Bay to shop. They while away time in informal visiting. Transistor radios are popular for entertainment inside the houses and teen-agers sometimes carry radios during their evening strolls. Few adults read regularly, and only one family subscribed to a newspaper and magazines. Comic books are popular with older children and are also popular as a pastime among fishermen.

Napping and "sleeping in" provide a pastime for everyone. Mothers in some households expect preschool children to take naps. Few villagers are either compulsive about sleeping or about not sleeping, particularly in terms of getting a certain number of hours of sleep at the same time each day. Young people who stay up too late and sleep late the next day may hear some criticism, but it is usually mild. Children stay up late if adults are partying or if there is any special excitement in the village or home. Teen-agers often boast of staying up all night or of plans to do so. Some parents insist on younger children getting to bed at a certain time, especially on a "school night." In summer when there is no school and daylight lasts until around 11 P.M. some children may be playing outside after ten o'clock while others have been hustled off to bed by 7:30 P.M.

Villagers are more sensitive to the environment than to the hour of the day in many of their activities, particularly those dependent upon tides. Tides favorable for clam digging, for hunting, or for travel along certain routes frequently dictate a rearrangement of mealtimes and of the hours of sleep. The fact that the tidal extremes occur almost an hour later each day literally puts the village on a twenty-five instead of a twenty-four hour cycle during clam digging periods.

During the fishing season many gill-net fishermen stay awake all night when their nets are out and sleep during the day when gill-net fishing is poorer. Packer crews sometimes work around the clock collecting fish from the seiners and gill-netters. A story is told of a local manager who fired a White packer crew when he found them all asleep after an exhausting number of hours of work; he replaced the crew with a native crew because, according to the story, "Indians don't need sleep."

CHILDREN'S ACTIVITIES

Young children are allowed and encouraged to help about the home but are almost never required to do so by a direct order. More is expected from the older children. Their tasks include chopping and carrying kindling, carrying water, tending infants, and hanging out laundry. Boys younger than about eleven are left to their own play and to the custody of the mother or older siblings. Walter and an older brother once went clam digging in order to earn money to buy track shoes, while another brother, younger by one year, did not join in because, according to Walter, he was "too baby."

The time immediately preceding and during early puberty is especially important for village boys. Most young teen-age boys like Walter receive more attention from their fathers at this age, they are frequently allowed to accompany and assist their parents, and they contribute significantly to the work of adult men. Older teen-age boys do not maintain this close co-worker relationship with their fathers, and they are less help to their parents than their younger teen-age brothers. Reggie and another young village boy received the kind of special attention usually reserved for older sons, probably because each of these boys was the first son and oldest child in his family.

Walter and his younger brother were almost inseparable. As a result the brother was able to participate in some activities in spite of his being "too baby," as Walter illustrates here:

> We went out jigging with my father and Raymond and it was blowing and we just came back. We went at 9:00 o'clock and we came back at 1:00 o'clock in the afternoon and all we did is just take our clothes off and jump into the water and we went for a picnic me and Raymond. We ate apple and sandwich and pop.

Walter's willingness and effort in school were similar to the diligence he displayed while helping his father. School attendance came first, yet Walter found it difficult to reconcile his meager accomplishments in class with the more vital help he might otherwise give to his father. During halibut fishing in May and June, Walter realized that if school were not in session he would certainly be out in the big skiff with his father. He wrote:

> I am going to go halibut fishing with my father and Raymond. That's why I asked you is there going to be school tomorrow because I want to go with my father. He always has a tough time when he catches halibut. We got one halibut yesterday.

Walter's cousin Joseph, fifteen, had grown into the more independent status of a young man. He seldom accompanied his parents, although he was often left in charge of younger siblings when his parents were away. Joseph and another boy his age decided to return to school during the fall, a decision which their parents approved but had not instigated. Just after the boys started school the clam season began and they were faced with the attraction of cash earnings compared to the satisfactions of the classroom. Joseph chose the writing period in class to tell the teacher that he intended to go digging:

> We are going to Gilford Island tomorrow I'm going to Stay there one week. I'm going to dig clams. There is a big tide this week. I'm not coming to School next week.

Once digging began, Joseph attended school intermittently for a few days and then he stopped attending altogether. In the months that followed he spent most of his time with relatives in a neighboring village, a move that increased his independence and resulted in fewer family demands on his earnings.

Dorothy's writing gives a good picture of the activities of a teen-age girl in a village home:

> Today is Friday. I am going straight home after school so I could do my house work. Then there won't be much to do tomorrow.

· · ·

> At noon I found a note on the table. It said, "To Dorothy. Hang up Damp Sheets. From Mom." It looks like my Dad's writing.

· · ·

> Today it is quite cold, besides being really dull. Looks like the weekend is going to be the same. I guess I'll just have to amuse myself with housework. Tomorrow I'll move my furniture around in my bedroom. My mom is supposed to wash today. I guess she'll be doing it tomorrow instead. I'll have to help her then. Well, I guess it won't be too dull around our house, with the washing machine running all day tomorrow. On Sunday I'll be ironing my clothes. Besides sewing some clothes.

· · ·

> Today when I was sweeping the front room floor my mom said I wasn't allowed to go to Alert Bay without her. She said, next thing she'll know I'll turn into a wild girl drinking and smoking. I don't know. I sure hate to miss "Follow That Dream," Elvis is acting in. Maybe she will go to Alert Bay to see my Granny in the hospital.
>
> This afternoon before the bell I was doing some embroidery on a pillowcase. I enjoy doing embroidery. Sometimes I'm in a mood to do embroidery work or read some comic books. I've finished all my library books. So I don't read a lot at times . . . This afterschool I am going to help my mom to hang clothes. My brother is going to scrub both kitchen and front-room floors after school.

· · ·

> Today I had lunch with Norma at their place, because the beans in our house would not cook. I had rice, with milk and sugar.
>
> My brother and I washed our hair last night. I took a bath last night too! After I washed and rinsed my hair, I went over to ask Beatrice to pin my hair up. She did, so I asked her to come and have tea with us last night. That's all. Hope it don't rain, it is cloudy.

When her parents were away fishing, she and her brother stayed at their grandmother's house. She wrote:

> My parents should be home in another four days. I sure am lonely for my mom and dad. I should be, I haven't seen them for eleven days!!
>
> I sure am anxious for September because I'm just tired of Blackfish Village. But in September I'll be in St. Michaels School.
>
> During summer looks like I'll be going to Rivers Inlet. I guess it will be all right as long as I get off Blackfish Island. Honestly I am tired of these boys here.

· · ·

Today is Friday. My brother and I sure are anxious for Monday. Because that is the day we are expecting my mom and dad to come home. I sure am lonely for them. I know now how it is going to be without my parents. Because I got so used to hearing my mom's voice. Shouting at me to get up at eight o'clock in the morning. I was so used to hear my dad's scolding voice when my brother did something wrong. I sure hope they stay home now.

Norma is older than Dorothy by one year. Norma is Dorothy's mother's youngest sister and thus is Dorothy's aunt. The two girls were constant companions. They are, however, a generation apart. Norma's position in her household, youngest daughter and a responsible teen-ager, found her helping her aging mother keep house for several older brothers as well as for three grandchildren living there. Norma once wrote as a brief description of her family: "I have four brothers and three sisters. They're all bossy."

Some excerpts from Norma's writing describe what she does and how she feels about it:

Tomorrow I am planning to clean up our house, it's like a pig house. Because nobody helps my mother when I am in school. Because my sister Beatrice is digging. She's trying to get money for Christmas for her kids.

. . .

My mother is washing clothes today. So I have to go straight home this after school. After I finish helping my mom, I'm going to play hide and seek. That's if some of the kids want to play.

My mother and I might go digging tonight. That's if she finished washing before I go home. I hope she finishes before I go home.

When I finish my dinner my mother starts yelling around. And I come to my sister's and she's yelling around too. I wonder if there's any place that's quiet around on earth.

. . .

Yesterday Dorothy's brother and I were washing my mother's jars. And we put it away. Then we washed the dishes. Then Alec came in the kitchen to cook supper. Then we had to wash dishes again. Gee! I got tired of washing dishes. I'm just going to walk out dinner time. So I won't wash the dishes.

. . .

Gee! My sister was really mad yesterday. She was spanking all the kids. She said everybody in the house is lazy. "You guys good for nothing. I feel like leaving you guys. You guys probably all go wild. This house probably turn into a pig house."

She was saying everything she could say. I feel like walking out of our house. But I don't know where to go. Live under our house. Maybe it's quieter under our house. Nobody yelling at me to do this and that. She was mad at me because I wouldn't help her when she was washing clothes yesterday. She isn't mad at me now though. She must of got up the right side of her bed.

. . .

Kitty and Alec came back from Alert Bay yesterday. Kitty was mad because none of us cleaned Alec's bedroom. Gee! She's a lazy old thing. Alec had to clean it up himself. And I guess Kitty told Alec to ask me to wash her clothes and iron them. But I didn't do it. Because she's got two hands. I got enough to wash my sister's kids, Richard and Weesa, and Tom's and my clothes. And the beddings. That's enough.

Dorothy and Norma occasionally played in the games of the younger children such as cowboys and Indians, but they took special roles ("queen of the cowboys," "Indian princess") which held the maximum dignity without requiring much overt participation. The younger teen-age boys organized running relays and boxing matches among themselves, they played hide-and-seek, and they chose "sides" for pursuit games such as cowboys and Indians, or Russians and Americans. A game called "horses," in which younger boys had to submit to being corralled and lassoed by older ones, drew criticism from one parent: "Those boys are too old to be playing games like that." Soccer and Indian baseball (a one-base softball game) are the most popular team games for boys and young men. Occasionally even the older girls joined in these games.

Social dances at the village are rare events. Few dances were held at the school during the year. However, any time a group of people gather for a drinking party there is likely to be a period of spontaneous dancing, and children may join in as their interest and coordination allow. Indian dancing and singing usually predominate in the parties which older people attend, while social dancing to music from a transistor radio or transistor record player are characteristic of parties where only young people are present. At one social dance held at the school Dorothy sat in the corner and read books the entire time, and Norma's only partner for the evening was an older sister. Yet later both girls remarked at what a good time they had and they pleaded for more dances.

Village parents do not share play activities with their older children but infants are held, bounced, talked to, and coddled. Only once during the year did I observe a parent at play with older children. The occasion was a lovely, lazy afternoon, and a young father was giving three of his children, the oldest age six, a ride in a wagon.

Adults neither organize nor instruct their children in play activities. For example, one day Reggie spotted a bicycle stored in his grandfather's basement and he asked his grandfather to take it outside for him because he could not get it out by himself. The bike had been purchased for Reggie's cousin, who had been unsuccessful in riding it. Without any assistance or direction Reggie set out to learn how to ride the bicycle. He fell off several times before he finally got it moving. After that his falls became less and less frequent. Reggie's father commented afterward, "He learned it all by himself. No one ever helped him."

Young children may play alone for brief periods but they are more inclined to follow after other children or adults nearby. Since every house is raised off the ground and therefore has steps at the front door (and back door if there is one), the steps act as a barrier to distinguish a house child from a yard child. Open doors or porches are often barricaded to keep crawling infants away from stairs and to prevent them from following older children out of the house.

The attraction of the shoreline offsets the attempts of parents to keep children entirely away from the water's edge, although villagers share the opinion that little children should not go unaccompanied to the deep water float over on the "other side." The beach in front of the village is not entirely visible from every spot in the village, and children have drowned at the beach and at the float. However, a parent can check more easily on the children when they are on the beach in front of the village.

On warmer days from April to October many of the children "go swimming." The beach is shallow in most tides and the children enjoy wading and playing in the water. Since the beach is also the garbage dump, broken glass abounds and children often cut themselves. Occasionally parents insist that children wear life jackets while playing in the water or along the water's edge. The children are not skillful swimmers and adults do not instruct them. A few children can swim in deeper water and do some diving. Children boast of swimming to distant points but usually stay close to shore. Boys are expected to be better than girls at swimming.

Older children enjoy rowing skiffs in front of the village or around to the "other side." Other activities of the older children include fishing from the floats, catching crabs, swinging on the set of backyard swings behind Reggie's grandfather's house, picking berries, riding one of the two bicycles, and, during 1962–1963, playing with the then-popular hula hoops.

The boys like to carry knives and do some carving. During one period the school-age boys made play bows and arrows which they used with considerable accuracy. At another time boys made slingshots, and the indiscriminate use made of them concerned adults. Reggie's grandfather asked the teacher on several occasions to remind the boys that according to village by-laws slingshots are not "legal" in the village. One afternoon none of the older boys showed up for school. They had seen the chief talking to the teacher at noon while they were at the beach using their slings. They assumed they were going to get in trouble, so they made a mass exit by rowing to another village. They did not return until supper time.

Some play is imitative of adults. Children imitate in play the activities they see about them and sometimes mimic adults' peculiar mannerisms. A favorite mime is acting drunk.

Boys play "lumberman" by walking along fallen logs on the hillside above the school, but since they have little idea of what lumbermen do they cannot elaborate on this play activity. Their greater firsthand knowledge of fishing has enabled them to develop a much more intricate game of "fisherman." Boats for this game are cardboard boxes which are pulled along the ground. In each boat is a long rope which represents the net. Another smaller box may be carried inside the larger box as a skiff. Combining (and confusing slightly) their knowledge of gill-net fishing and of purse seining, the children play the fishing game by throwing out one end of the line and running in a straight line or in a huge semicircle letting the "net" pull out of the boat to make the set. The play-fisherman then gets into the box and pretends to sleep while the fish come in. The net is pulled into the boat in the hand-over-hand manner used by the men. When the net and skiff are back in the box, the play-fisherman pulls his boat along the road or across the soccer field to make another set. When the boys want tangible evidence of fish, they scoop a handful of gravel from the road to put in the box. Like the men, their references to the catch are by number: "I got 200 that time." A boy without a "boat" can be an airplane representing the watchful eye of the Fish Commission. A play-commissioner flies about and arrests everyone as a matter of routine.

Reggie's six-year-old cousin was playing at fishing one afternoon when I was walking along the road. He wanted to continue his game but he also wanted to accompany me. He decided to do both by running alongside me and making a straight set along the road which he dragged behind him as we walked together. "I'm only going to make one set," he explained. "I don't feel much like working today."

In their play the children are not inclined to explore the island beyond the trails running through the berry vines at the back of the houses. Walking within the village is confined almost exclusively to the road and the paths between houses. To take a stroll, villagers traverse the length of the road several times.

During the long hours of winter darkness and on rainy days, indoor play activities are important. Toys do not last long but there are toys or parts of toys in every house. Playpens have rattles and plastic toys. Children enjoy crayons and coloring books; crayons disappeared regularly from school. The children play card games like old maid and donkey. Older teenagers are good at cribbage, also a favorite game among adult fishermen. One boy had a set of Monopoly. Checkers and dominoes are played as long as new sets remain intact. Radio listening is as popular among the older children as among adults, and several teen-agers collect records of popular hit tunes.

Events like holidays and birthdays do not ordinarily receive special attention. I was told that possibly once in his childhood and once in his teens a child might have a birthday party, but otherwise the occasion is apt to be dismissed as casually as in this account by one boy:

> My birthday is today. And I am 13 years old today. My mother said "Happy Birthday, son."

Few daily adult activities go unnoticed or unobserved by the children. Whenever the adults are busy with their tasks one can expect to find a child or group of children watching the work or playing nearby. If groups of adults are busy canning, barbecuing, or visiting, the children are literally underfoot. At times an adult becomes exasperated with so many children around as he attempts to work, and children may be told: "Go play!" Yet even the forbidden "other side" becomes tacitly within limits if an adult is there working on a net or an engine.

When children are addressed for purposes of discipline or direction, the typical village parent does not often speak loudly or harshly; rarely does an Indian adult scream and shout at his own children and I have never heard an adult speak harshly to a child not related to him. One of the most frequently heard phrases for admonishing children is "Don't fool around." The phrase is often repeated with no change in inflection. One mother used the phrase so often in addressing her children that it had become a monologue. The admonishment seldom produced any immediate response.

Perhaps because there were so many adults in his grandfather's home, Reggie seemed to receive a constant barrage of warnings and admonitions. No matter in what manner each adult directed him, the phrases were inevitably repeated. His parents usually cautioned him by saying, "Reggie, don't do that," or just said his name drawn out in one long "Reggieeeee." One uncle usually discouraged Reggie's presence with "You kids get away from here now," a warning Reggie seldom heeded at the first hearing. Another uncle was inclined to ignore Reggie's presence or behavior until Reggie got himself into some minor predicament, whereupon the uncle would deliver almost the same spiel regardless of the occasion: "That's why we never take you—you always fool around too much. You get into everything, climb all over the place, start things up when you shouldn't touch them. You really act stupid."

Reggie was threatened occasionally with a spanking, but the spanking itself almost never materialized. At times he and his cousin were sent to bed during the day as a disciplinary measure. This seemed to be the maximum punishment used by Reggie's grandmother, and her criterion for using it was if the boys had been *"really* naughty," such as playing on the beach and returning home wet and muddy. Sending the boys to bed was effective and possible in her house, but the large families and small houses make such a measure almost impossible for most parents. Village children are occasionally confined to their homes as a disciplinary measure.

Parents tend to be more realistic than idealistic in resolving conflicts among their offspring. Bigger and stronger children are not expected to treat smaller siblings as equals. If a young child complains at the treatment he receives, his mother is quite likely to tell him not to bother the older children if he cannot get along with them. Bullying is treated somewhat as a fact of life, and the child who is bullied is generally considered to be at fault. Some parents expressed concern over the bullying their children received by other village children but their only direct action was to complain to the teacher. As a classroom problem, bullying is discussed in Part Two.

2 / The annual economic cycle

THE DOMINANT economic activity of the villagers varies with the season, and the importance of any particular economic activity varies with each individual household as well. If village men thought of themselves in terms of a predominant occupation, they would characterize themselves as fishermen; this is the most frequent entry made by or for them in any official document. But the same occupational roles are common to most village men and they do not tend to think of themselves by vocation. Identity comes from one's family and band, not one's job.

Fishing is the dominant economic activity from June through October. Clam digging begins after fishing and continues commercially into March. Spring time activities include local fishing for cod and halibut, and a few people still assemble each spring to catch eulachon and to prepare eulachon grease. Preparations for commercial fishing increase gradually during the latter part of spring. Then the cycle repeats. Logging and heavy construction jobs are occasionally available throughout the year.

CLAM DIGGING

Digging is the primary source of immediate cash. A clam digger needs only a pail, a clam fork, and, for nighttime digging, a lantern. Clam beds are numerous. The most accessible beds are dug over too frequently and serious diggers travel to more distant spots. Villagers who travel far to dig may remain away during the entire period of a digging tide, about nine days. Sacks of clams are collected daily during the digging tides by the clam buyer, a member of a local band. Cash is paid each time the buyer picks up clams. The buyer also extends credit so families may charge digging equipment or purchase staple food items from him in advance.

Clams are dug in the "big" tides when high and low water levels are at extremes. Local tides vary as much as 22 feet. The best tides for digging are the "zero" tides and tides of 1 and 2 feet. Such low tides occur at night during the fall and in daylight during the spring. Every period of big tides is followed by a period of tides too high at low water to expose the sandy intertidal zone where the clams are dug. Locally tides are dichotomized during the digging season as "big tides" and "no-good tides."

Digging is a family enterprise in most households. In earlier days digging was considered women's work. Men do most of the digging today but, by the very nature of the work, they find little to boast about except after an exceptionally good day. Their complaints are many: there aren't as many clams now as there once were, the clams are getting smaller, too many people are digging, the price is too low ($1.80 was the rate per 60 pound box in 1962–1963).

A neighboring village has served as the center for local clam digging for many years. During digging season some people from Blackfish live temporarily at this village. As the clam center, this village takes an important position in the winter economy, while Blackfish Village lacks the advantage of being at the hub of this or any other economic activity.

Almost two million pounds of clams are dug annually and transported to Vancouver for processing. There has been talk among the officials of the Native Brotherhood[1] of building and operating a cooperative plant to process locally-dug clams on a profit-sharing basis. People in the outlying villages express little interest in the idea of a cooperative, for they recognize that the employment opportunities will not affect them and no one has been willing to guarantee that the digger will receive more *cash* for his clams.

The clam buyer is literally the only native with whom the villagers have cash dealings. Because of his prominent position the complaints about him are legion: he does not pay enough for the clams, he does not come when he says he will, he is getting rich while everyone else does the work, he charges too much for the things he brings around on the boat, and so forth. Yet for all the complaints most village adults and some children dig clams for at least a few tides each season. The sound of the horn announcing the buyer's approach often brought requests from the older boys in class to be excused so they could sell clams dug the evening before. Some children missed days of school during the better digging tides.

Digging is a key source of income for Walter's family, and his parents reportedly make up to $200 per tide. Walter's older siblings often dig with their parents but Walter did not join the digging except during school vacations. While not all families work as hard at digging as Walter's, villagers have a reputation for digging at least a few sacks of clams in every tide. At the digging tide which occurred during Christmas week only Blackfish Villagers dug. When the buyer discovered that only one village had been out digging he commented, "They're hungry over at Blackfish."

More villagers dig in February and March when digging tides occur in daylight. By the end of the commercial clam season in March 1963, nearly every able-bodied adult in the village was digging. One family recruited an older son from school during the final week of digging so he could help pay off money owed to the buyer. The teacher received this note:

---

[1] The Native Brotherhood of British Columbia is an Indian organization whose activities today are primarily concerned with Indian fishermen, although membership is open to all Indians in the province and ostensibly any problems of the Indian people are within its domain.

Blackfish Village, B.C.

sign by
Dan
Alfred

"Hello There"

Andrew is not coming to school today I mean Half a day please thank you. Well the reason why I want Andrew to go to dig cliams to pay our order in cliams buying please

THANK
YOU

When clam digging stops, jobs and money become scarce until fishing begins.

SPRINGTIME ACTIVITIES

Springtime activities include some opportunity for selling bottom fish like halibut and cod to cash buyers. Hunting, digging, and fishing for household use are important subsistence activities at this time. Reggie's grandparents, always the most active in keeping a full larder, engaged all available adult members of the family in one three-day period to dig and put up clams for family use for the coming year.

The lengthening and warming days of springtime find an increase in outdoor activity. Some efforts at spring housecleaning coincided with an official proclamation for an all-village clean up. The councillors of the village posted two handwritten notices along the road:

Spring Clean Up

Rack All Gardens
Burn All Rubbish

No great flurry of activity resulted from the posting of the notices, although Reggie's father spent two days raking and cleaning up around his father-in-law's house, already one of the best-cared-for houses in the village. It was not the notices that spurred Reggie's father, he explained, but his dislike of "just sitting around with nothing to do." The signs were torn down by the children after two days.

The eulachon has historically been the harbinger of spring for the Kwakiutl. Each spring the eulachon make their run up the inlets into the fresh waters of the Canadian mainland. During this season, the Indian peoples all along the coast converge near the river mouths to catch the eulachon and to prepare grease. There is still individual and local pride in making good grease, and people argue about whose grease is best among households, villages, and regions. One native from an area to the north said with cautious criticism that the grease made by the people around Alert Bay was "very different" from that made by his people.

People from Blackfish Village join other local villagers at a shared site at the head of Knight Inlet to make grease. No one from Blackfish Village made grease in the spring of 1963, although one group of villagers did make a brief visit to the head of the inlet to catch several tons of fresh eulachon which were brought back and given to any villagers who wanted them for cooking and smoking. Grease-making is a time- and energy-consuming task which requires catching the eulachon in nets, carrying tons of fish to huge pits where they are left to decompose for ten days, and then rendering the grease in huge vats of boiling water. Fewer families make grease each year and there is a growing market among village families and people at Alert Bay for the grease produced. School attendance prevents most Indian children from ever observing and participating in this traditional subsistence activity.

LOGGING

A widely shared opinion among those concerned with the present and future economic development of the British Columbia Indian population is that logging holds the greatest employment potential for Indian labor. This potential employment does not represent an absolute increase in the number of jobs in the lumber industry. As with fishing, technological improvement has meant increased total output with a decreasing labor force. The potential employment for the Indian population is a function of location. Logging operations are moving farther from urban centers and, thus, in many instances, nearer to the isolated areas where natives comprise the only locally available labor supply.

There are several logging camps in the Blackfish region ranging in size from one-man ("gyppo") operations to very large-scale ones. The largest local operation during 1962–1963 was a camp then terminating years of seasonal activity. The camp was within commuting distance of the village (twenty minutes by a skiff with an outboard motor or "kicker"), and two villagers made the daily trip for a brief period.

Logging has some features which make it similar to fishing and attractive as a form of work to Indian men. It is outdoor work with good pay and the elements of risk and adventure lend excitement. Among some villagers the guarantees and job benefits (such as minimum day's wage guarantee if equipment breaks down) are a source of wonder and a fulfillment of the idea of the economic good life: "You get paid even if you don't do nothin' that whole day." Yet few villagers consider logging as a source of employment and income for themselves. Neither of the two village men who worked at logging thinks of himself as a logger first or foremost.

Even among neighboring villages where more men are experienced loggers it is a rare individual who chooses a logging job or who stays on the job once fishing starts. Reggie's father and uncle Arnold, the two village loggers, always take jobs on seine crews at the beginning of the salmon season. Like all fishermen, each anticipates that *this* summer will be the one when he will make enough money so that he will not have to work during the rest of the year. Fishing represents the "big chance" each year. Reflecting on the poor catch for one season, Arnold said, "Well, it looks like I'll have to go into the woods again this winter."

The steady employment of logging makes it unattractive to many natives. Fishing has its long weekends or occasional tie-ups so a man can stop to enjoy his good earnings. On a logging job a man is likely to earn far more than his immediate cash requirements, yet he may not have a chance to enjoy his earnings unless he gives himself a holiday. Arnold has a habit of taking such holidays, and consequently he finds new jobs only in camps where the management is unaware of his reputation or where a camp is so shorthanded they will take a seasoned logger even though he is known to be unreliable. This generally unfavorable reputation is an occupational stereotype of Indian loggers. The only logging position for any of the other villagers during the year was a short-term job for three men booming up logs after one camp closed for the season.

Reggie's father was able to go logging immediately upon his arrival at the village in February but when his camp closed a few weeks later he searched in vain for another logging job. His in-laws sympathized with his inability to find a job and complained that Indian loggers are usually the last hired and first fired. When a bunk house at a small camp burned down during the spring, word spread that the camp was hiring local Indians. "There's no place for White guys to stay there, so now they'll hire Indians," was the reaction.

Other reasons keep village men from logging. Unlike fishing, where a boy has some firsthand information about the nature of the work from his earliest youth, there is no opportunity to observe exactly what loggers do unless one joins them. Some villagers expressed their hesitancy to take logging jobs because they did not know what would be expected of them, how hard they would have to work, or how much real danger they would face. Another problem in logging employment is that full-time work usually requires moving about as camps open and close. Except for the company which operated a camp locally, no camp is near enough to the village that the men can return home each evening. Bunk house accommodations are all that are available. Village men do not like enforced separation from their families and they express no interest in logging or construction jobs that necessitate living away.

Another factor complicating logging work relationships (although potentially a problem in all work-group alignments) is the problem of White foremen supervising Indian men. As already noted, villagers generally refrain from telling others what to do and in turn look with disfavor on anyone who acts "bossy." In the work group of the logging camp, White loggers accept the authority of a foreman; Indians often do not. There are many ways to cope with overbearing authority. Before a teacher, judge, or agent an Indian may hang his head. If a logging boss issues too-sharp commands or attempts to blame him for a foul-up, the Indian logger is apt to walk off the job right then. Many Indian loggers have done so. They derive satisfaction from telling the stories about when they quit and "how surprised that guy was."

VILLAGERS AS LOGGERS

Reggie's father and uncle Arnold are experienced loggers. Both men are more acculturated to White ways than the average villager and both enjoy their associations with Whites. Concomitantly both men are somewhat socially marginal to village life, the father because he belongs to another band, the uncle because of interpersonal problems with fellow villagers, particularly when he has been drinking. The marginal status of Reggie's uncle is further aggravated by the almost total social isolation of his wife from village women because she is from outside the local area and is a common-law wife. I diverge here to discuss these two men and their families because they illustrate the problems for natives who become transitional between village life and a way of life more characteristic of the dominant society. The relationship of Reggie and his family to the school is discussed in Part Two.

Reggie's mother is a member of a large village family, a family that plays an important role in contemporary village life. Her father has served as chief councillor of the village and has been a council member ever since the formal chief and council system were introduced at Blackfish Village. He owns a seine boat, one of his sons is a skipper of a seine boat, and all his other sons, including Arnold, are fishermen. A former Indian agent said of the family, "They are the only family at the village who is worth a damn." It was certainly true that if any official visitor to the village was going farther than the school (most did not), he visited Reggie's grandfather's house. The family home is the center of family activity, and during the year all the children, grandchildren and great-grandchildren spent some time visiting. When visits overlapped, the household was overwhelmed by children and adults.

Reggie's parents have spent most of their married life in Reggie's father's village although they had returned to Blackfish Village for several long periods when Reggie's father was out of work. Such was the occasion for their return to the village in February. When a logging camp where he had worked for several months shut down, Reggie's father was unable to find another job. Without a steady income there was no way the family could meet their rent payments and feed and clothe their four children. They particularly wanted their son to be well dressed during his first year in public school.

Reggie's father referred to his year's income from fishing, $2400, as a "low year," but his earnings from logging during the fall, an additional $1800, kept him solvent until the camp shut down. Like most Indian families, this family spends their income as it is earned, buying what they consider "the best" in food and clothing: "We ate pretty good—steak every other night." When the weekly earnings stopped, they were without any resources for meeting their living expenses. When Reggie's father received a heavy fine in court for trouble which arose out of a drinking spree, he and his wife returned to the village once again. If this time they were more reluctant than usual, it was because they preferred to keep their son in the provincial school.

Reggie missed only one day of school in transferring, and his father was at work at the local logging camp on his second day back at the village. The only other villager employed at the time was Arnold. The two men commuted to the camp to earn $18 a day and $30 on Saturdays. Reggie's father worked steadily until the camp closed for the season. Then he started a long search for work.

Reggie's father is a friendly, easy person to meet. When he is worried he becomes reticent, and during his weeks of unemployment he often became quite uncommunicative. He expressed concern about his income and occasionally complained that worry kept him from sleeping. In moods of depression he contemplated where he might take his family so that he could provide for them.

He generally avoided liquor since his recent trouble with the law occurred when he had been drinking. Along with his court fine, he had been temporarily "interdicted," a legal status in which one is prohibited from purchasing or consuming alcoholic beverages. He recounted how he sometimes got into trouble when he went to have just one beer because he had so many friends and they all insisted that he join them for a beer. "I guess I must have an overwhelming personality," he explained.

The physical features of Reggie's father—his height, his angular face in contrast to rather characteristic roundness, his light complexion—all tend to minimize his Indianness and may facilitate his acceptance by Whites. Before liquor "opened up" for Indians in British Columbia he claims he could pass for White anywhere he was not known personally.

Reggie's father is proud of his seventh grade education. He skipped the sixth grade and still managed to get "just about a perfect report card." He left school in order to earn money. He once made arrangements to reenter school in grade nine, but he did not return from fishing in time. He laments that he did not go further or take advantage of other training opportunities available to Indian youths. In discussing his own education he said he felt that now, in his late twenties, he was too old to get training and too burdened with family responsibilities. He believed that now he would have to pay for the training while when he was younger the Indian Affairs Branch would have paid for it.[2]

Reggie's mother and father are among the few village parents who have rather specific aspirations for their children. They think Reggie should, and will, finish high school and hope he will be a skilled worker of some kind "like a mechanic or TV repairman." As a six-year-old, Reggie thought he would like to be a policeman. Reggie's present fascination with his grandfather's seine boat and with everything about fishing does not lead his father to conclude that Reggie will be a fisherman. As he explained, "Reggie does like to be around boats but that's natural for kids."

Although Reggie had to finish his first year of school at the village his parents were determined not to have him continue in school there nor to start his sister's education at the village. At times they expressed other dissatisfactions with village life. Discussing the stress in interpersonal relations among some villagers, Reggie's father said, "There's so much hate here." His wife commented, "It seems like every time we come back here this place is a little worse. It will never change." They anticipated leaving the village as soon as their resources permitted.

Like Reggie's father, Arnold identifies with both White and Indian cultures. However, as he attempts to reconcile two cultures into one life style, Arnold evidences more personality disorientation than does his brother-in-law. Arnold's parents have always enjoyed good relationships with Whites, but Arnold has lived most of his life at Blackfish Village. He has had far less opportunity than Reggie's father to experience a wide variety of contacts with White people. His contacts have been limited mostly to work groups and to drinking parties.

---

[2] His information on this point was inaccurate. Villagers often had misinformation or misperceptions about opportunities available to them, about their rights, and about their medical problems. The attempt has been made in this study to present situations as villagers perceive them. In the present example Reggie's father still considered taking specialized training "some day" though he thought he would have to finance such training entirely on his own. When, two years later, he did take a special course, the Branch not only paid his tuition but also gave him an allowance for his family.

Arnold often leaves the village for extended periods of time, sometimes taking his family but more often leaving them while he goes off on a logging job. Ultimately he returns to his home and family after he quits a job, starts partying, and subsequently runs out of money. His drinking is a continual concern to his parents, wife, and children.

Arnold usually begins each summer as a crew member on his father's boat and he remains with the crew at least through part of the season. As both a fisherman and a logger, he likes to think of himself as a "real highball guy"—a fast and strong worker. As a crew member he once described himself as "the best man on the boat . . . and the worst on the weekends." He gets along easily with Whites and enjoys being on logging crews with them.

During those times between jobs when he was at the village Arnold often expressed discontent with his present status and an accompanying hopelessness about what to do or where to go to improve his situation. His comments reflected his feelings of ambivalence about being an Indian and about remaining at the village. Contemplating entering their young children in school, Arnold and his wife expressed their desire to have them attend a better school than the one at the village, but they made no move to bring this about. I inquired about his aspirations for his son's schooling. He explained, "I'm going to make him stay in there. And in the summer I will teach him about fishing and logging and he's really going to work."

Arnold's vascillation between a commitment to his Indian heritage and his aspirations toward the dominant society is reflected in a variety of behavioral patterns and attitudes. Watching a group of children at play on the shore of a little lake one afternoon, Arnold noted how the Indian children and White children separated into two distinct play groups along the beach. He commented:

It's the same on the beach at Vancouver. When we go there with the kids, we always sit right in the middle between the Indians and the Whites.

FISHING

A large and predominantly Indian fishing fleet, including many gill-netters and twenty-eight seine boats, operates out of Alert Bay. In late spring seine boat skippers reenlist former crew members, some of whom work on the same boat year after year, and select new crew members from among the large group of relatively unskilled men and older boys. Many Indian fishermen move from crew to crew during each season and gradually drift away from fishing as weekly catches diminish in the fall. By the end of the season, during the fall fishing, some skippers go out with only part of a crew and occasionally a skipper is so shorthanded that he must remain tied up for the week.

Skippers and senior crew members have some opportunity for employment in the late spring working in the net lofts and bringing company boats from Vancouver. The amount of preparation has decreased steadily over past years since newer materials, particularly nylon nets, demand less maintenance and repair. Except for special tasks like painting a privately-owned seine boat, there is no employment for new crew members until the fishing begins.

Villagers, like all local fishermen, pursue either gill-net fishing or purse seining with a strong allegiance to one or the other. Gill-netting is basically a one-man operation in which fish get caught (gilled) in the net. When the fisherman takes in his net at the stern of his small boat, he removes the fish from the net one at a time. Purse seining requires a larger boat and net and takes up to a seven-man crew

Children watching the mending of a seine net.

to make and close a set, take up the huge net, and, following a good set, to brail the fish into the hold.

The catch on a seine boat has to be far greater than that of a gill-net boat to return comparable earnings and meet the expenses of equipment and operation. Seine crewmen work on a share basis, dividing profits after fuel and food costs are deducted. The top earnings about which I heard rumors, the combined shares of an Indian skipper and his wife (who was aboard as cook) were said to be over $40,000 for one recent "really good" season. In actuality, crew shares average about $2,000 per season, but hope and talk of huge earnings are ever present. As I left the village to accompany a seine crew for the first time two of the older school boys asked me where I was going. When I said I was going fishing, one of them commented, "Boy, Mr. Wolcott, you gonna be a millionaire."

The village is unusual in having few gill-netters and in having three seine-boat skippers. Crew positions on the village seine boats are filled first by family, then by friends, then by local villagers, and finally by "outsiders" from other villages or by Whites. All three village skippers take women cooks from their own families. All three have experienced difficulty with hiring "village boys" because they are not dependable. Not until the season progresses and crew replacements are harder to find do the skippers usually decide to give young men from other village households "another chance."

The fishermen argue and compare the merits of the fishing companies with which they deal but they generally remain with the same company year after year. Company managers return this loyalty by allowing gill-netters the use of their boats for a long period, by selecting local fishermen as skippers of company-owned seine boats, by offering financial support and advances when earnings are inadequate, and, sometimes, by paying court fines. Some fishermen just manage to break even after the season but the companies continue to help them. There is a pattern of paternalism toward Indians among both public and private agencies that deal with them, and the fishing companies follow the pattern.

Complaints about the fishing industry and the growing problems in it for Indian fishermen are widespread. A paraphrase of the complaints is a reflection of the way many villagers view not only the fishing but their whole way of life:

> "It's not as good as it used to be."
> "It's OK now, I guess."
> "There's no future in it."

Changes within the fishing industry are gradual, and men who feel that their young sons will need other occupational skills in the future see no immediate threat to their own work. Their pessimism concerns the long-range outlook rather than the immediate future. For example, shortly after a poor season, Reggie's mother wrote:

> Reggie's father was lucky to make a few dollars all right. But fishing was pretty poor this year. Perhaps next season will be the good one that they were expecting this year.

Villagers have witnessed remarkable changes in fishing technology, in government conservation policies and regulations, in the declining Indian participation in British Columbia's $70,000,000-a-year (1963) fishing industry, and in the subjugation of their own organization, the Native Brotherhood, to the powerful United Fishermen and Allied Workers Union. Complaints heard today include: there are too many boats; other fishermen, especially sport fishermen, are taking an increasing proportion of the total salmon catch; and the government "isn't doing what it should" for the fishermen. Local fishermen are concerned about the offshore fishing of Japanese and Russian fleets and about the constantly decreasing number of total fishing days allowed because of conservation practices. In the 1962 season fishing was limited to four days a week; in addition five tie-ups were called during which no fishing was allowed for ten consecutive days. A long strike in 1963 effectively took care of conserving the sockeye run that year. The philosophy prevailing in 1964 and 1965 held that it was better for the fishermen to go out regularly each week even if for only a limited time. A policy of a forty-eight-hour fishing week was inaugurated. Fishing opened at 6 P.M. Sunday and closed at 6 P.M. Tuesday, leaving a minimum of four completely idle days during each work week.

Village adults have already experienced a major technological change that totally displaced local Indian women in the fish canning industry. Not too many years ago local fishing required local facilities for canning, and the bays and inlets between Vancouver and Prince Rupert are dotted with deserted canneries. All locally-caught fish are now processed in Vancouver. In the earlier days the Indian women were as important to the fishing industry as the men, and the fact that the canneries were dependent upon the wives and daughters gave the men an excellent bargaining position in requesting company boats and supplies. Today processing provides no employment for local Indian women. Except for the few women who cook on the seine boats or who mend nets, women are no longer part of the labor force.

The decrease in jobs for the men has been less dramatic but over the years the jobs on the seine boats that require the sheer brute force of a large crew have gradually disappeared. Lines and nets that were pulled by hand are now pulled by power winches and power blocks, and boats that go out "short" a crew member or two find no handicap in routine operations. For several years local fishermen have been considering the use of drum seiners, boats which use a smaller seine net handled by means of a huge drum at the stern. For the 1965 season several local purse-seine boats were converted to drum seiners. A crew of four men can operate a drum seiner. Although the net is smaller, the speed and ease of making and taking in a set allow a drum-seine crew to make many more sets per day. If drum seiners are the coming thing—and even skeptical native skippers contemplate how much easier it would be to find three rather than six crew members after a five-day weekend—then the young, unseasoned fishermen may have increasing difficulty obtaining jobs. Coupled with this prospect of a steadily diminishing labor market in their major occupation is the estimate that by 1975 the Indian population of British Columbia will be doubled.

VILLAGERS AS FISHERMEN

The summer activity in the households of the children who receive special focus in this study illustrates the relationships between specific villagers and the fishing industry.

Reggie's grandfather is an owner-operator of a seine boat and is one of the senior skippers in the area. Compared with other local seine boats, his catch is described as "good, but not among the best," meaning that he is a steady fisherman but only occasionally is his a "high" boat. He likes to point out that many skippers in the local fleet, including most skippers of high boats, "all got their start on my boat." Of the group of ten village men who had jobs on seine boats when the season opened, eight are members of Reggie's grandfather's family either by birth or by marriage.

By the time little Reggie is old enough to work legally on a seine crew (sixteen) he will probably have spent part of every season for the previous ten years on his grandfather's boat. As a six-year-old he had already learned how to do some of the tasks. Whether in ten years his grandfather will still be operating such a big boat is another question, a thought that has already crossed his mind. Cruising the inland waterways one day we spotted a small seiner which operates with a three-man crew and always remains in the protected areas. "Some day, when I'm an old man," said Reggie's grandfather, "I'm going to get a boat like that. And then I'll go fishing out here, with just Reggie and his cousin for my crew."

In Joseph's household two older brothers and his father are experienced fishermen. Joseph himself lacked only a month of being old enough to join a crew when the season opened. Joseph is a big, strong boy, and had anyone in his immediate family been skipper of a boat he would have been assured of a job. Without a job, Joseph's summer in the village passed very slowly. There were few people around other than the women and little children. There were almost no opportunities to leave the village. Joseph felt that he was better off not to go to Alert Bay and risk getting drunk and getting into trouble with the RCMP. He confined his partying to the village, either by joining drinking parties when others returned to the village with liquor or by "sucking gas," a practice of inhaling fumes from a rag soaked with naphtha (lamp gas) popular among teen-age village boys.

By mid-July Joseph seemed overcome with boredom as he contemplated whether anything would ever happen to change his circumstances. He heard about the possibility of going away from the village to continue his schooling, and he asked my advice about writing a letter of inquiry. With three tries and an hour's work, this is the letter he drafted to the regional superintendent of Indian Schools:

Dear Sir

My name is Joseph Willie. Iam sixteen years old and I would like you to help me to back to school. I would like to go school down Vancouver. I was in Grade six when I quit school. I would like to make money befor I go how much money do you think I need to go down there. I havent saved any money yet I maybe able to save some if I get a job on one of them boats what if I don't make any money would you be able to help me go down.

I would really like to go down Vancouver to go school so I was wondering if you would help me.

Yours Truly

/s/ Joseph J. Willie

The answer was "Sorry." The superintendent explained in a letter to me that there was no program then for intermediate grade dropouts. There was an accelerated program for students who had completed grade eight, but, he wrote, "Joseph would not have a chance in the existing program." On Joseph's behalf I investigated two other possible ways he might attend a residential school. He told me he was even willing to be in a sixth grade classroom as long as it was not at Alert Bay where he knew everyone. I felt that what he wanted most was an opportunity to get away from the village and, if possible, to get to Vancouver, since a girl friend from a neighboring village had been accepted for a special vocational program there. None of the alternatives worked, and Joseph did not leave the village. The last time I saw him in the village in 1963 he was walking aimlessly along the road with another teenager and three young school boys. He was carrying a half-consumed case of beer in one hand, a can of lamp gas and a rag in the other. The youngsters shared the beer as it was passed around.

Exactly a year later Joesph repeated his plea for help in going away to school. He had not proved to be a steady worker on a crew and had not held a steady job during the fishing season. There was still no school program available for him although there were better prospects for such a program. Joseph's only accomplishment for the year was that he had stayed out of jail.

One of Joseph's older brothers had a job on a seine crew when fishing began in 1963; his oldest brother and his father were in jail. Joseph's father hoped to operate a gill-net boat after he was released. Although Joseph's father is experienced at both gill-netting and seining, he was unable to find any fishing job, and no company would give him a boat. Villagers say he is a good fisherman but that when he has money he gets into trouble over drinking. Eventually Reggie's grandfather hired him on his crew. "How else can he feed that big family?" he pondered, perhaps to rationalize his previous declaration that during this season he was not going to hire any more villagers.

Walter's father, like Joseph's is a seasoned fisherman. Using his large skiff he was one of the first villagers fishing for cod and halibut in the spring. Like Joseph's father he has a reputation for letting his drinking interfere with his work, although he and his sons are considered excellent crew members when sober. The year before, Walter's father had worked a short while on one boat from the village, then he "jumped" his boat, withdrew his total earnings ($600), and went on a three-week bender. No village skipper felt like employing him for the season, although he was occasionally hired to help mend nets at the village.

If Walter's father had been a skipper, Walter would have had an opportunity to be on a boat. In the following season, Walter's father did arrange for him to accompany him on a seine crew, although he had never provided such an opportunity for his other sons. Walter took his role as crewman very seriously, even joining the other crewmen in complaining about their lazy cook. The next summer Walter proved to be such a valuable crew member that his skipper "cut him in" on the shares. Like other village boys in their early teens, Walter is willing and eager to work with the men and to be treated like them; in fact, he is more serious about it than most. In the same serious vein two of Walter's older brothers who have reputations for being excellent workers voice their concern about not letting their drinking interfere with their fishing. Walter says that he is not going to drink when he grows up; he also boasts about the occasions when he has been drinking.

Dorothy's father, Frank, a gill-netter, was the first villager to fish commercially in the 1963 season. He had been without a boat most of the previous winter while the engine was being rebuilt. Without the boat he was free from the obligation of transporting his wife and his in-laws but he was also limited in his own freedom to travel, visit, or seek employment. Shortly before the fishing season his boat was ready.

Frank and his wife insisted on regular school attendance for Dorothy and her brother, but with many relatives living in the village they showed little concern about staying home to look after their children. As soon as they had the use of the boat, Frank and his wife took a series of local trips that kept them away from the village for days at a time. The children were unhappy at being left behind to go to school. Dorothy's brother wrote:

> My mother and father never once stay home. They just come in and leave the next day. They just came from Kelsey Bay. They stayed all week. They came last night, took a bath, and left for Alert Bay today. Looks like I haven't got a chance to say hi then you have to say good-bye.

Frank's wife often joined him in fishing. She stated that she wished to spend as little time in the village as possible. The parents were away so long on one occasion that they sent food to their children via another boat, and Dorothy wrote:

> I hear that my mother has moved to Alert Bay but she hasn't told me about it and she hasn't even come for her clothes.

Frank began commercial fishing in May. Dorothy recorded at the time:

> My father left early this morning to go halibut fishing up north. Yesterday my father sawed some wood for us. He probably won't be back for ten days.

Word of good salmon fishing prompted Frank's journey to other local waters. Dorothy wrote:

> Yesterday my dad, mom, and James [an older man who was fishing with Frank] were on their way to Kingcome Inlet. They went to Kingcome Inlet to fish. My dad's relative Norman got two hundred and seventy dollars in two days. When Norman saw my dad at Alert Bay he asked him to go try fishing at Kingcome Inlet too! My dad will also see lots of his relatives over at Kingcome Inlet too! My dad, mom, and James should be home on Thursday or Friday. Sure hope they get lots of fish.
>
> They are fishing for the Indian Sports Day and for our spending money. They also fishing for my C.O.D. at Minstrel Island P.O. My C.O.D. costs ten dollars and ninety-nine cents.

Toward the end of school in late June both children were eager to leave the village and spend the summer fishing. Most local gill-netters start their summer fishing in Rivers Inlet, off Queen Charlotte Sound, a long two-day trip from the village. In a good season some gill-netters spend their whole summer "at Rivers." Every major fishing company has fish camps there at old cannery sites where net lofts, stores, fueling stations, showers, and sometimes repair facilities are maintained. Bootleg liquor and parties are part of weekend camp life for many. The fish camps become annual summer residences for the Indian, White and Japanese fishermen. The fishermen of each ethnic group tend to moor their boats among others of the same group.

During the spring Frank's wife said she wished that she could go away to work in a cannery for the summer, but her husband would not allow her to do so. Her next hope was that the family would stay at Rivers Inlet and get one of the one-room houses, complete with shower, that the company lets its fishermen and their families use during the season. These facilities were originally built for the cannery workers, and the shower was one of the main attractions for Frank's wife.

In June Dorothy's brother wrote in class:

> Ten more days until we go to Rivers. We are going after school on the 27th because there is lots of fish at Rivers. My father could have gone there, but he's got to wait for Dorothy and I to going out of school.

In past years some children from the village had been taken out of school before it closed in June in order to accompany their parents for the opening of fishing. Because he waited until his children finished their school year, Frank missed out on a fair week of fishing. By the time he arrived with his family all the houses were taken. The family spent the summer on the boat.

While visiting one day with Frank I asked him what he thought his son would be when he grew up. He said he had asked him but the boy did not seem to know. He doubted that his son would remain at the village. I asked Frank if he felt that the boy knew very much about gill-netting. Frank responded enthusiastically, "He knows just about everything there is to know." For their daughter, Frank and his wife held vague aspirations complicated by her continued success in school. As for their son, regardless of whatever else he may do, he will also be a gill-netter.

Many Indian gill-netters operate marginally. While they have a low overhead in running their slow old boats, breakdowns and the inability to move quickly to better fishing during the short fishing week make these marginal fishermen poor competitors among the gill-net fleet. A good gill-netter, with fishing skill and modern equipment, may make more in a season than a seine-boat skipper. Seine crewmen discuss the "easy" life of the gill-netters, the simplicity of their fishing operation, and the freedom they have from bosses. Gill-netters are not without their problems, however. Indian people do not like to work alone or to be alone, yet gill-netting is essentially a one-man operation and hiring a crewman is a luxury. Indian gill-netters frequently take their wives and families, an arrangement that can produce tensions in the confined quarters of the boat and conflicts between the fisherman's work and his obligations to his family.

Strikes, such as the disastrous three-week strike during the 1963 fishing season, are a problem for all fishermen. Frank provides a good example of the effect of the strike on a gill-net fisherman. He had waited until school closed before taking his family north for the important sockeye run. By doing so he missed the first part of the run. After two "weeks" of fishing, a total of four days, a strike was called. Frank, like most gill-netters, remained at Rivers Inlet hoping daily that the strike would end. After the peak of the run, with still no strike settlement in sight, Frank returned to the village. His earnings from his brief period of fishing had been exhausted in maintaining his family away from home during the strike. The family stayed overnight at their village home and then made the long trip south to the Fraser River, near Vancouver, hoping to catch the last of the sockeye run reported there. By the time he got there, that run, too, was over. All Frank had to show for six days of travel were his fuel bills.

Perhaps because Dorothy and her brother are so close in age and because there are only the two children, the family does a great deal together. The ties between parents and children in their family are unusually close and life on the small boat provides the children with intimate models of adult life at work and leisure, sober and partying, and for the range of moods each parent exhibits. Just as her brother has learned "just about everything there is to know" about gill-netting, Dorothy has learned the appropriate feminine role on the boat. Unlike some White women who join their husbands at fishing, Indian women make little effort to be competent mariners. They may cook and they may take the wheel during a long trip or while the net is being taken up, but the operation of a boat is considered the work of a man. While Dorothy's parents have encouraged her attendance at school and have occasionally talked of a different kind of life for her, the role she knows best is that of the woman in a gill-net fisherman's family.

AUGMENTING RESOURCES

Fishing, clam digging, and logging dominate the cash economy of the village but there are other resources that are important to all villagers.

Direct employment by the Indian agent or the Indian Affairs Branch is one possible source of income. Reggie's father was the only person to hold a regular job for several weeks with the Branch, but small construction projects at the school provided a few dollars for five other village men during the year. Young village women often have an opportunity to earn money scrubbing and cleaning the school at the end of each summer.

Hauling materials from Alert Bay to the village school and to other villages is another source of income. Reggie's grandfather has a reputation as one of the dependable skippers for such work. He is well paid for these charters, although he also hauls many supplies for the school and teacher without charge. Friction results because of this special source of income, with accusations from villagers that he "makes money off the school." Confronted with such charges he points out the many services he provides at no cost and insists, "We never get paid nothing for all that we do."

Sale of mink and otter pelts provided income for three households, and one young husband boasted that he was making fairly good "wages" by his hunting prowess. Trapping was not a regular source of income among villagers during the year although in other villages trapping provides important income and trap lines are checked regularly.

On a few occasions in past years Reggie's grandfather has chartered his boat to White sportsmen, a source of income he would like very much to develop if he knew how to go about it. He is also intrigued by business deals, and he has loaned money to both Indians and Whites. His loans are made in good faith for he has little recourse when someone does not repay.

Subsistence activities themselves produce surpluses salable to both Indian and non-Indian buyers. In addition to the occasional presence of a cash buyer for fish there are local markets for crabs and abalone. Eulachon grease brings a good price even at the village. Some canned salmon caught for "own use" is occasionally sold to strangers although most villagers restrict canning to household use and for gifts. Criticism was voiced about one family that obviously canned salmon far in excess of its own needs. There is some borrowing of food among households; however, borrowing is usually restricted to relatives. Grease and canned salmon are the only food items sold among villagers.

"Home cooking" sales were held by the village women to raise money for the all-village parties at Halloween and Christmas. Otherwise baked goods were usually exchanged rather than sold except to outsiders like the teacher or to the school maintenance crew.

In the form in which they are carried out today the potlatch gatherings provide a minor source of cash and goods. As part of the ceremony, along with speeches, dancing, and eating, the host of a potlatch customarily gives money to male guests, with an announcement proclaiming each gift of a large bill ($20, $10, or $5) and a final gift of a one- or two-dollar bill to each adult male. Other gifts may include basins, pans, china, towels, aprons, linen, gallons of eulachon grease, and a seemingly endless supply of sandwiches, apples, oranges, and cakes. The scale and significance of potlatching has altered considerably from the great giveaways that adults remember in their younger days. Yet the events themselves are exciting social occasions and everyone anticipates the Indian dancing, the refreshments, and the possibility of receiving gifts and cash. Somewhat disappointed at having received only one gift at a gathering that lasted from midafternoon until midnight, Dorothy's brother mused while returning to the village, "That's an awful long time to sit for just one plate."

In its day potlatching provided an institutionalized means for redistributing surpluses. It put a high value on "getting one's name up." A man exchanged goods for status. The accumulation of goods beyond one's immediate needs was a prior step to distributing them. At the potlatch one literally heaped upon one's fellows a combination of goods and obligations. In the White man's economy the accumulation of goods is an end in itself. Villagers who accept the White man's system have found no easy compromise between the old way and the new. In accumulating personal possessions one invites the incessant pressures of immediate family, relatives, and fellow villagers for loans or gifts of goods and cash, for loans of equipment, and for rides and other favors. To comply means one's resources are constantly being threatened or actually drained; to deny the requests and to hoard resources is to risk both having things taken anyway and being called "stingy."

Some villagers seem conscientiously to have avoided accumulating wealth or possessions. For example, one of the events in world news during the year was the account of a threatened invasion of North America via Cuba. Reflecting on the remote possibility of a threat to Blackfish Village, Dorothy's father revealed his philosophy about accumulating material wealth: "Well, if they come here, they won't get anything from me because I don't have anything." In a recurring pattern he has seen that any time he has a few dollars on hand his wife or some other relative asks him for money. To "get ahead" and stay there is virtually impossible while living in such close proximity to one's kinsmen and one's fellow villagers. The few families who have accumulated many personal possessions—even such things as extra clothing, costume jewelry, or home-canned goods—worry about them constantly. The villagers who have been most successful in acquiring material goods moved away from the village long ago.

Within the lives of the older people another activity has been of some importance as a dependable source of income—prostitution. Historical accounts suggest that during their early contact with Whites the Kwakiutl were rather pragmatic about prostitution. The growth of the city of Victoria, following the Fraser River gold rush in 1858, provided an access to city life for the Kwakiutl, and they began to look to Victoria as a source of excitement and as a source of income from employment and prostitution. A winter trip to Victoria became an annual event for many women; the money earned by prostitution was turned over to the husband to aid him in his potlatching.

In recollecting about village life for women in that earlier day a missionary woman who lived at the village recounted in a personal communication:

> According to the Indian code a woman might earn money from men to hand over to her husband to make him a big man. I knew one who when I knew her was a charming Christian woman, a great help in the missionary group. I was told that she had been one of a group that went down to town every winter.
>
> The Indian husbands used to go to meet the boats bringing the women back, to quarrel about the money. The married Indian man bought his wife and the woman had to pay back the money. When she had paid back the money she could leave him if she wished—she need not. . . . Things had changed a lot in my time and I expect more in yours.

Today the liquor, money, and great number of unattached males moving through Alert Bay encourage sexual laxity, particularly when parties grow so naturally out of the beer parlor's easy conviviality. Local prostitution is not institutionalized and partying is a more common precursor to the bestowing of sexual favors than is a direct cash offer. It is not unknown for a woman or someone else in the house to "roll" her partner when he spends the night with her, a difficult charge to prove when, as typically happens, the male has been drinking heavily and there are other adults and children wandering about the house. The precaution to being rolled is simple—a man spends whatever money he has in the beer parlor first. A young man complained about a village woman: "Darn that Maggie. Every time you sleep with her she rolls you."

The production and sale of native art work provide some income in the region but not at the village. Many Vancouver stores sell Indian art and crafts, and some shops specialize in such merchandise. Buyers insist that there is a ready market for Kwakiutl painting and carving of good quality. It would seem that villagers might develop handicrafts as a cottage industry, yet only one mask, quickly carved and of poor quality, was produced at the village during the year. The repeated visits of artifact hunters have already depleted village households of masks, rattles, whistles, and button blankets handed down from earlier generations. The few remaining items are not for sale.

The standard explanation why so few people produce art work commercially today is that without the stories and dances they helped to symbolize, the art forms lack meaning. Whether this is the real reason that no villager today does any serious carving or painting, I do not know. Masks I bought from a carver in another village received some criticism when I showed them to villagers: "It's not supposed to be that way," or "He put so little hair [cedar bark] on it that it looks like a White guy." Some of the older teen-agers can draw excellent designs and sketches in the highly stylized manner of Northwest Indian art, particularly of the killer whale and of the thunderbird, but their efforts are for pastime only.

A one-time source of revenue for individual villagers and for the collective band fund was a logging operation some years ago on reserve land. In the local style of logging every timber that could be taken was cut, and today the logged area behind the village is only a dense mat of scrub brush and undergrowth. Villagers express little interest with band lands or with band monies. They experience little say in their management. As to the lands themselves, villagers sometimes philosophize that *all* the land really belongs to them. The Kwakiutl, like most British Columbia Indians, have never signed a formal government treaty. Agitated occasionally by this unresolved "land question," the people enjoy talking about a settlement day when all British Columbia land will rightfully revert back to the native population. "I ask myself, 'What are all these White guys doing around here anyway?' " said a prominent member of the Nimpkish Band. Or people dream of a day when each Indian will get a huge sum of money, his share of the settlement, as villagers have heard that Indians in the United States have received. At other times villagers take a different view of the land question: "They could take all this away from us anytime they want." The Indians feel the same way about their band funds. The agent solicits the signatures of band council members when money is needed for routine expenses, but in their attempt to reelectrify the village the councillors were thwarted in their wish to spend existing funds. Because the agent, on advice from Branch engineers, recommended against the expenditure, the three councillors could not bring the issue to a vote. The band fund is a source of collective wealth over which villagers feel they have almost no control.

Another way to augment one's resources is to take what belongs to another. Some villagers stole goods with such skill that in any other context their efforts would have warranted a host of terms more often used to epitomize the noblest traits of primitive Indian life: cunning, daring, stealth, resourcefulness, and even parsimony regarding what was taken. Among villagers the range of attitudes about personal property varies as to how inviolable it is, how intensely one feels toward another who steals, and what can be taken under certain conditions. The lack of consensus concerns what can be taken, not the taking itself. Everyone complained about everyone else. One villager once said of another:

> That guy can steal anything. You'll be standing there talking to him and all of a sudden you realize he's chewing your gum and you didn't even know it was out of your mouth.

For some villagers actual possession is the only essential determinant of ownership, and even among the young children the challenge, "Hey, that's mine" is usually met with a reflexive, "Prove it." With any object a person acquires comes the obligation to watch out for it as long as he really cares about it. In homes where people have acquired things they consider valuable, doors can be locked but the preference is to have a member of the family remain at the house whenever possible. "You lock you door even if you only going to walk down to the float," the chief councillor advised me.

Stealing is too strong a term for some of the borrowing that goes on. Tools, equipment, and skiffs are borrowed and then not returned to the place where they were found originally. Fuel is frequently taken from boats, usually in small amounts but sometimes to the extent that a fisherman suddenly finds himself adrift while on a trip or else he cannot even depart. Trap lines and crab traps were poached even by relatives. Clothes, particularly stockings, were taken off clothes lines. Food disappeared from outdoor coolers and sometimes from kitchens. Fuel was taken from the school as frequently as once a day during the winter. Several houses and the school were broken into during the year. The seclusion and distance from the watchful eye of the RCMP also makes the village a good hideaway for boats, motors, and guns stolen elsewhere, and several such objects were once discovered cached in the attic of a vacant house.

The activity surrounding stealing is not hidden from the children in those households where it is a frequent practice. Indeed, the young sons of one family not only accompanied their father in some of his purloining but were sent by themselves on minor forays such as taking fuel oil from the school. Younger children in that family boasted openly of acquisitions made by their elders. Intrafamily stealing was a problem among children, and the schoolroom was a favorite hiding place for objects taken from other members of the household.

GOVERNMENT SUBSIDY

The total cash income received by the members of every village household includes government funds. The availability of such subsidy money results in a subtle dilemma resolved differently by different families: whether at one extreme to minimize one's own resources and ability to earn an income, thereby maximizing one's dependence, or, at the other extreme, to eschew any special help or favor and to maintain relative independence.

All families in Canada receive a monthly Family Allowance paid on the basis of the number and age of dependent children. The Family Allowance entitlement ranged from $6 to $8 per child. While such a payment is small for the urban parent with his high expenses and small family, the size and importance of the Family Allowance check for six village families made it the biggest single source of dependable and recurring income.

With a family of ten children, Joseph's parents received the largest Family Allowance benefit check. His parents were usually "away for a few days" each month when the check was expected in Alert Bay. The lack of care Joseph's parents showed for their children drew frequent criticism from some other villagers, and the monthly trip to "drink up the Family Allowance" drew the greatest criticism of all. Not infrequently Joseph's parents were accompanied by other parents who were expecting checks. Not on every occasion did they return to the village drunk and broke; often they returned with boxes and boxes of "grub." On such occasions their critics insisted that if they took better care of their family this is the way they would return every month.

Unemployment insurance provides a source of income in some households. Village fishermen consider their unemployment money as deferred earnings rather than as a source of emergency income. Crew members occasionally find at the end of a season that they have not worked enough weeks to be eligible for later benefits. Under such circumstances they may complete their eligibility during clam digging. Because of the casual way clams are sold, villagers can manipulate their sales to maximize everyone's benefits under the unemployment insurance program.

Compensation benefits provide the majority of the income for one village household. When Norma's father was killed several years ago in a fishing accident, the compensation board awarded her mother a monthly payment of $160 plus $20 for each dependent child. A regular monthly check of $200 sustains the whole household quite adequately. With her large and dependable source of income, no one in the family has to work and no one does. Her sons, Norma's older brothers, hunt or dig when they feel like it. They occasionally work on seine crews. Although they often complain of their boredom, the life they lead seems idyllic to some of their younger nephews. I asked one nephew, an eleven-year-old, what he wants to be when he grows up. He answered, "A drink man." I asked him if he wants to be a fisherman. "No," he said. "I'm just gonna sit around like my uncle. He never does anything. He gets paid in a check."

Direct welfare payments made by the Indian agent provide the only subsidy income that is special for Indians. The only difference between relief obtained by Indians through an Indian agent and the assistance available to non-Indians through the provincial welfare department is in the flexible and generally lower scale the Indian agents use in granting relief benefits. Increasing dissatisfaction with this dual system, which Indian spokesmen hailed as a blatant example of economic discrimination, led to the recent adoption of a more standardized scale for all welfare payments.

Filing a one-page form available at the agent's office initiates the application for welfare assistance. During 1963 the agent used the following scale for determining the maximum monthly assistance for a family: no contribution for rent, $22 for the head-of-household, $15 for persons over twelve years of age, and $12 for children age twelve and younger. Agents do not necessarily give out the maximum welfare. Regardless of the circumstances or of his intent, if an agent decides to discipline a family economically he risks criticism by native people within his agency and he risks the possibility of an unfavorable account by the press. Agents sensitive to the effect of welfare in keeping people economically dependent find the task of distributing equitable welfare doles both difficult and distressing. Some agents meet any request for help by giving the maximum allowable; some relinquish their personal involvement and delegate the responsibility of assigning welfare payments to an assistant. The mismanagement of funds, particularly in connection with handling and distributing welfare monies, seems to be an occupational hazard among Indian agents. A generalized notion of mistrust toward agents on the part of many Indian people is periodically reinforced both by stories they circulate among themselves and by the occasional official announcement of the sudden transfer or dismissal of an agent. It was under such conditions that a new agent was appointed during the field study.

One village family was almost totally dependent on welfare. The agent required the father to perform certain jobs about the village if he wished to receive a full dole, such tasks to be supervised by the chief councillor. In the agent's rationale, this meant that the man was "earning" his dole; he would have been surprised to learn that the man sometimes took a son out of class to help with the work. Other relief payments tended to be for specific occasions or circumstances. One such circumstance that prevailed rather frequently was when a male head-of-household received a short jail sentence which left his family without a breadwinner. During the year this happened in three village households, with the irony that while a villager was in jail both he and his family enjoyed a higher standard of living than was possible when he was home. If attitudes toward asking for and receiving welfare help are transmitted like other attitudes, then different values about dependency are being learned by children in different village families. In Reggie's grandfather's house the idea of seeking regular welfare is literally unthinkable; to some village families the idea of not seeking aid is equally unthinkable.

3 / Social activities of villagers

COMPLEMENTING THE ACTIVITIES of daily village life and of the major annual activities are certain social activities which recur over time but which are not routine activities occurring regularly each day or week. Such activities include formal social gatherings, drinking, sports events, travel, religious activities, and formal band activities. These activities and a brief discussion of social control are included in this section.

FORMAL SOCIAL GATHERINGS

Several social gatherings, the contemporary form of the traditional potlatches, were held during the year. The practice of giving away or destroying more than one's rival has undergone considerable modification,[1] although gift-giving (described previously) is still an important part of these occasions. Villagers refer to these gatherings as "Indian dances." Most of the Indian dances held during the year were at Alert Bay. Two dances were held in neighboring villages, one on the occasion of a wedding, the second, a memorial.

These gatherings have formal and informal aspects. One traditional aspect is the speechmaking in formal Kwakwala dialect. Few people are both fluent in the proper dialect and knowledgeable in the traditional protocol for conducting the speechmaking. The young people say that they cannot understand the formal dialect. When I asked what was being said during the speechmaking, a young man answered, "I haven't got a clue." The old people insist that the knowledge of proper potlatching is dying out.

The rhythm and songs for the dances which follow the speechmaking are usually provided by a group of the older men who sit in two rows facing each other chanting the songs and beating a rhythm on a plank. The dances originate from a real or imagined offstage area behind the musicians to which dancers return at the conclusion of their dance. Most of the dances are performed by men. They wear carved face masks and capes made of skins or cedar bark as the dance requires. The women sit along the sidelines and occasionally stand to sing and to dance in place, swinging their shoulders and hands from side to side. The costume which the

[1] Helen Codere has provided a historical account of changes in potlatching in *Fighting with Property: A Study of Kwakiutl Potlatching and Warfare, 1792–1930* (1950).

54

An Indian dance held at a neighboring village. (Courtesy of R. P. Rohner.)

women add to their regular dress is the button blanket, a heavy blanket with buttons sewed on to form a design.

The dance participants include novices and experienced dancers. The prior experience of the young dancers may be limited to drinking parties in which they have tried the dances or to practice sessions immediately preceding the formal gathering. In practice sessions they are not likely to receive instruction or criticism from their elders. One young man was very enthusiastic about participating in the dances, but he also voiced his frustration in trying to learn his dance, for no one would tell him what he was doing wrong, no one would correct him, no one would criticize. He commented, "Even if you ask, they might not tell you anything."

One potlatch dance attended by many villagers accompanied a formal Anglican church wedding. The ceremonial speechmaking, gift-giving, and dancing were referred to as the "Indian wedding," the native complement to the official Christian ceremony which preceded it. The formal activity of the Indian wedding was followed by an evening of social dancing to music provided by a combo made up of men from the host village. Other informal aspects of the gatherings include visiting, partying, and a gamut of interpersonal relationships ranging from the hospitality extended toward distant relatives to the encounters of the young people, with the almost inevitable threats or fighting among the young men. A village teen-ager wrote his version of the activities which followed the wedding:

So we got all dressed for the dance. About 9:30 when we got in the fun. Yeah men we had fun. we damn near "Twisted" all night. If they didn't stop the orchestra. And I twist my soles of my shoes of. I had to sit down for awhile until I got a knife to cut it off.

About 12:30 we had a little beef with some of those village boys. After the dance we all went home to find a place to sleep.

We went to Frank's Aunty's house to sleep. We didn't sleep until about six in the morning and we had to get up at 10:30 in the morning. We went in to have some coffee. After that we went straight to the Hall to go watch the Indian dance. After dance I got four dollars from the man who gave money out.

Potlatching as a way to validate personal status is no longer universally shared and recognized. However, the potlatches today do provide a means for validating group identity, for demonstrating commitment to the old ways, and for noting a socially significant event such as a wedding or the giving of an additional Indian name. Highly acculturated Indian people in Alert Bay join with members of the surrounding villages and participate with enthusiasm in Indian dances. Adults are ambivalent about potlatching. Those who have given potlatches argue that "it doesn't do any good," yet everyone tries to attend the gatherings and there are occasional hints at the possibility of giving one. Villagers are uncertain of the legal status of potlatches today and are chary of the opinion that an activity which has been in violation of the law for most of their lives is now officially encouraged. While the dances are held infrequently, there is little doubt of their impact on village children for whom the activity is one of the few big occasions and one of the distinctly Indian ones.

DRINKING

Problems associated with drinking pose some concern to every household in the village and are of major concern for one or more members in ten village families. During the period of the fieldwork alcohol was involved in all but one of the ten deaths among villagers, in all serious fights, in most accidents (including six cases which required hospitalization), in two cases of hospitalization in which drinking aggravated existing medical problems, and directly or indirectly in all but one jail sentence. One couple for whom drinking became an increasingly severe problem during the year finally separated and attributed the cause to drinking. The behavior of villagers while drinking also revealed latent hostilities and feelings of aggressiveness toward other villagers, toward family, and toward White people among natives whose nondrinking behavior gave no hint of such feelings.

In its pleasanter aspects drinking provides a means of increasing sociability and releasing feelings that otherwise tend to remain pent up and unverbalized. Village partying can be jovial, friendly, and relaxing. Drinking can take the edge off inhibitions and find a characteristically shy and reticent people participating enthusiastically in conversation and in impromptu Indian dancing and singing. Drinking is "feeling good."

Village parties start anytime, any day, although they are least apt to occur on Sunday when liquor cannot be purchased. Wine and beer are the usual stimulants. Parties are not community affairs where anyone is welcome, although the invitation to join someone for a "little drink" may be as succinct as, "C'mere." A villager always finds someone to drink with him before he begins drinking. Close relatives or friends may be allowed to join a party in progress, but there is some uneasiness if a party grows too large for the available amount of liquor. Doors that are not usually locked may be locked during a party, and an exclusive "Don't let anybody else in" may be heard among partying villagers who otherwise never talk in such terms.

The social purpose of drinking—to get "feelin' good" or "feelin' happy"—is a condition that can usually be achieved on precisely the amount of liquor available. For younger males the epitome of a good party is to "pass out" from drinking and such experiences are the cause of some boasting. "Passing out" carries no connotation of drinking to excess, but rather suggests a mellow state where the participant becomes so relaxed that he falls asleep. Such behavior is considered inappropriate for women whose husbands drink heavily and who therefore feel they are responsible for protecting themselves from passes made by other men.

For years some local Indian leaders have held the opinion that if the Indian people could have equal drinking rights with Whites the problems and covert nature of Indian drinking, including a considerable business in bootlegging, would disappear. The combination in the summer of 1962 of opening a liquor store at Alert Bay, a new interpretation of the laws resulting in equal purchasing rights for British Columbia Indians, and a good fishing season provided a sudden and unanticipated opportunity to see what consequences these changes would have. Many Indian people felt things were getting worse as the year progressed while some felt that the drinking problem was not any more serious than it always had been.

There is a generally shared idea among Indians and Whites about Indian drinking behavior that, as a prominent Indian man expressed it, "Once an Indian gets that stuff in him he can't stop, and he goes back to his old ways and starts to dance around and go haywire." The idea of "going haywire" means that if the liquor results in a man acting or behaving badly, the fault is in the alcohol, not in the man, and he cannot reasonably be held accountable for what he does under its influence. "Was I bad?" asks a village man the morning after a party. "He couldn't help it, he was drunk," explain his relatives in his defense.

Many wives of men in their thirties and forties express concern about their husbands' drinking and its disruptive influence in the family. Older Indian men share the concern about drinking as a growing problem and decry the drinking of their own middle-aged sons. Often these same men have been heavy drinkers in the past but now are moderate drinkers or abstain completely. If their own motives are to provide nondrinking models for their sons, they never expressly state it.

Drinking provides an incentive for earning money and thus for finding work; for a few individuals money has almost no other use. Payday includes a drinking party for most villagers, and anticipation of a future party provides relief from tedious work. During a long, slow morning on the seine boat one crewman announced, "Harry, the next time we get to Alert Bay I'm going to buy forty bottles of wine." One problem with drinking as an incentive for earning money is that the partying that follows payday may result in a failure to return to work.

The quietest periods at the village were those when no one had a job and consequently there was no extra cash for liquor. Reggie's grandfather claimed that the village is a better place to live when everyone is broke, for then parents stay home with their children and there is no drinking. One village woman was almost hysterical after her husband went on a binge one evening and she spent the night fleeing and hiding from him throughout the village. "I don't think I can stand another fishing season with him," she said. "All he does is drink when he has the money."

SPORTS EVENTS

Soccer is the favorite game in the village and there is often a group of teen-age boys kicking a ball around on the small village playfield. School boys played soccer at many recesses and were often joined in such games by older boys who no longer attended school. Younger boys are sometimes allowed to play, especially if they act as "goalie" to chase into the bushes after the ball. Most soccer games consist of a group of teen-age boys divided into two teams both kicking toward the one existing goal post. The men cite their ability to "still play a good game" as evidence of good physical condition.

If so many of the men had not been in jail during the spring (for a while there were nine), the village might have fielded a soccer team to play in the intervillage competition as it has done in some past years. Two village players did complement another village's team in competition. The winning team among the outlying villages plays the Alert Bay team during the annual June Sports celebration. Beside the games themselves, the intervillage events provide some excitement and travel for children and adults and the bigger celebrations include relays and competitions for everyone. Most village adults and all but three school children attended the three-day Sports at Alert Bay. That celebration concluded with soccer playoffs on Sunday. The next day only two children had returned to the village for school.

Some village teams have uniforms, coaches, workouts, and even training schedules. Blackfish villagers have apparently been unsuccessful in effecting team discipline. Village "boys" are reputed to be good, fast players but are criticized because they cannot sustain their effort for the duration of a game and are poor losers. A man who had coached a team in another village said, "You just can't tell those Blackfish boys anything—they do it their own way or they get mad about it. They've got to be tough and independent."

Attempts of well-meaning teachers to capitalize on intervillage sports events by organizing interschool competition have not been successful. One teacher attempted to organize a softball game between two village schools. A factor that prevented the game from becoming an annual event was the negative effect on the children, adults, and teacher in the neighboring village when the Blackfish team adopted the slogan: "If we can't beat them, we'll beat them up."

TRAVEL

Villagers spend a lot of time in local travelling. While travel is regarded as routine, actually getting from place to place is always a slightly unique event. The predominant mode of travel is by boat. A person who has no boat of his own "hops a ride" on a boat going where he wishes to go. It is virtually unknown for someone to refuse to give a ride to those who request it just at the moment of departure, although misinformation may be given about when or whether the departure will take place. An uninvited rider has few rights and few obligations. As one villager commented, "You give these people a free ride to Alert Bay all the time, and when you get there they don't even thank you or help you tie up."

Reggie's grandfather was the only villager who had a dependable source of transportation throughout the year. He often provided the only link between the village and Alert Bay. During the nonfishing times he usually made a weekly trip to the Bay, and villagers who wanted to hop a ride kept a close watch for him on the day of his customary trip for food and mail. Four villagers had the use of gillnet boats for varying periods of time although none of these boats was available all year. Boats from neighboring villages and from Alert Bay also provided transportation for villagers, especially during the fishing season.

Men travel more than women, although several women drew criticism for constantly being away when they should have been looking after their children. Only one older woman showed any fear of boat travel; she rarely left the village. Reggie's grandmother's family joked that it is hard to get her to leave the house to come on the boat, but once she is on the boat it is equally difficult to get her to come back to her village home.

The chance to make a trip to the Bay or to travel anywhere is an opportunity no child wants to miss. Children denied a chance to accompany parents on a trip made their resentment evident in school. One of the youngest children in class succeeded in crying and running out of the classroom any time he saw his family preparing to leave for Alert Bay. The family always relented and let him join them although by the end of the year the boy boasted that he was "a big boy now" and he no longer cried or begged to be taken along if he was in school.

Travel provides an important element of variety for children and adults and even young children complain if they have to stay at the village for long uninterrupted periods. Travel usually is associated with good times. For adults the trips often culminate in parties either at Alert Bay or when they return to the village; many trips are made expressly for liquor. For children the trips include possible opportunities to buy ice cream or candy treats, have "Coke and chips" at the café, see a movie, and visit friends. Children also enjoy accompanying adults shopping, since adults are indulgent and an easy touch for a dime or quarter. For the teen-agers, trips mean a chance to hear the latest recordings in the cafés, to see their movie idols at the theatre, to meet other teen-agers, and, sometimes, to party.

Under some conditions, children are not allowed to travel. Regardless of the intent, few round trips are made by villagers in a single day. Unless a trip starts on Saturday the problem of missing school is frequently given as an excuse for leaving children at the village. Often parents do not want to be encumbered with their children during anticipated partying, and they do not take younger children unless there is an older child along who can look after them. In the families where a trip invariably results in drinking and remaining away for several days the children accept the absence as routine. Brief written comments made by a village girl on two succeeding days illustrate the matter-of-factness with which children may regard their parent's absences:

My mother went to Alert Bay with my father but they are going to come back today. They just went to get the Family Allowance.

. . .

My mother didn't come back yesterday. Maybe they were too drunk with my uncle and my father too.

RELIGIOUS ACTIVITIES

"This is a tremendously over-served population," concluded a visiting missionary after making a survey of the medical and missionary needs of the outlying villages. A similar comment is often voiced by local doctors, nurses, and clergy. Occasionally representatives of several different services arrive in a tiny village on the same day and literally outnumber the population they have come to serve. A local clergyman learned during a conversation with me while I was visiting in another village that his stop at Blackfish Village on the following day would coincide with a visit planned by another religious group. Realizing that the two groups would arrive at the same hour, he inquired good-humoredly, "Well, whose side are *you* going to be on?"

A reasonable guess as to the occupation of any White stranger visiting in the village is that he is a religious worker (second guess: the Watkins' Home Products man). Religion is imported in the village; during the course of the year six different Protestant groups provided activities ranging from a one-hour film to a three-week Daily Vacation Bible School. Religious workers may draw a sizeable audience if there is no competing activity in the village, especially if the program includes refreshments or a novelty like colored slides or an accordion accompanist.

The most active missionary work during the year was sponsored by the Pentecostal Church. White Pentecostal workers lived in two neighboring villages, and one of these workers held a weekly meeting (weather permitting) at Blackfish Village to a congregation usually consisting of all the children and a few adults. The service included action songs popular with the children. A few hymns have been translated into Kwakwala and printed in song books provided at the service. The best-attended religious meeting of the year occurred when a native Pentecostal group from Bella Coola presented an afternoon service with music (including accordion, electric guitar, and drums), testimonies, prayers, and a sermon.

The parents of an eight-year-old village boy reported proudly that their son was "saved" at that meeting and that he had accepted the challenge to "give his life to the work of the Lord." They were very proud of this boy, their eldest son. They confided their own hope that the boy might become a doctor but when the boy was "saved" the parents said that his becoming a minister would be all right. They asked whether it took very long to become a minister, for they hoped the boy would go to high school. The boy's mother had experienced a long indoctrination into Anglican Christianity during her childhood at the Anglican residence school and in the Anglican-affiliated tuberculosis preventorium established at Alert Bay. While she expressed doubt that she was living a "good Christian life" herself she did feel she was raising her children by Christian precepts. She described her eight-year-old son as "a real Christian boy." She often used the terms "good" and "bad" in discussing behavior with her children. She explained to them that one major reason for avoiding bad behavior is that none of their actions ever goes unnoticed: "I may not always see you, but God sees you."

The Kwakiutl have had Anglican instruction for over eighty years although Roman Catholic missionaries were the first to introduce Christianity in the region. Older adults who had any schooling attended the Anglican school at Alert Bay in an era when religious teachings were central to the instructional program. Today villagers are usually baptized, married, and buried with Christian blessings. Christian beliefs receive official sanction in provincial schools through a prescribed daily reading from the Bible and the recitation of a prayer.

An official ruling requires all non-Indians, including missionaries, to secure permission from the band council before visiting or presenting a program in a village. Reggie's grandfather, as chief councillor, always granted permission to visitors at Blackfish Village. I asked him if he felt the missionary visits of such a variety of religious workers weakened the ties with the officially-recognized church. He answered, "We're all Anglican here. Those guys can come around if they want to."

Religious interest and commitment among families vary widely. The general assessment by former religious workers is that as a group villagers seem little affected by Christian ideals. One team of summer religious workers noted what they termed "coolness toward the Gospel" on behalf of villagers, and in their written summary they concluded: "The group appeared well versed in Bible stories, Bible language, and salvation, but their lives don't prove it."

Religious activity has varied greatly during the last forty years but no activity had been indigenous. Each period of activity has been dependent upon some outsider and has varied with his energy, his enthusiasm, and his tenure. The policy of the Anglican Church to concentrate its efforts in a few villages rather than to try to serve them all led to comments by villagers that they were being "forgotten," although only a few children and not one adult attended an Anglican Communion that was offered at the village.

For the children who remain at the village all year the Daily Vacation Bible School, held for many summers, has been a source of religious instruction and a welcome variation in the summer routine. The "DVBS" schools are operated by the Marine Medical Mission, an interdenominational organization which has served native coastal people for years. Initially their ministrations were more medical in nature; recently the activities have focused on Christian teachings. The team members who conduct the two or three week daily Bible school are usually Bible college students preparing for missionary service. Teams are placed in villages along the entire British Columbia coast, and there are more requests for their services than can be met. The annual return of a DVBS team to Blackfish Village reflects a combination of the enthusiastic response of some families and the summary recommendations submitted by team after team that in spite of difficulties with the children and the indifference of many adults, this is the kind of village which can benefit by Christian instruction.

Fifteen years have elapsed since the departure of the self-appointed missionary to the village who lived there for twenty-two years and who was instrumental in initiating religious, medical, and educational programs at Blackfish Village. Because her efforts were so central in opening a school in the village, her influence is discussed in Part Two.

BAND ACTIVITIES

The village is formally organized into a band with three elected councillors, one of whom serves as the chief councillor. The same people tend to be reelected term after term. In some villages there are women councillors, and a woman has occasionally been elected chief councillor, but Blackfish villagers have always elected men. Band council organization had been in effect in the village for eight years at the time of the study. Reggie's grandfather had always been a member of the council and was serving his second term as chief councillor. Dorothy's father was elected to the council that year, a position he had held before. During an election meeting both Walter's father and Joseph's mother were nominated for the council but declined. Villagers typically decline.

In the fall the chief councillor called two evening band meetings. Most adults present in the village attended. Business was conducted almost exclusively in Kwakwala. One major item of business was a discussion about collecting money for the Halloween party and the Christmas "concert," parties traditionally given at the schoolhouse for the entire village. Both parties require expenditures for food and prizes. The Christmas party customarily includes the presentation of a gift to each child. Selection, wrapping, and tagging gifts is done by a Vancouver department store. For the large number of children in the village (it was estimated that sixty-five presents were needed) and for the time needed to fill the order, the chief councillor wanted to "get the people thinkin' about it" early in the fall to have a nice Christmas party "for our dear children."

Villagers launched their fund raising in a unique way. The school has a coal furnace and requires an annual shipment of coal to the village. Twenty tons were delivered on the wharf in September. There the coal remained—200 sacks of it. The agent offered $80 for the job of carrying the coal up to the school but there were no takers. Reggie's grandfather thought of moving the coal as a community project to earn money for the Christmas fund. He discussed his plan with the teacher and directed the teacher to "Go ask Dorothy's father. He gets the people organized for something like that. Tell him it was my idea." Dorothy's father agreed that the idea was a good one. Weeks went by without further comment or action. One day two wheelbarrows were borrowed from another village. Next, boards were laid on top of the gravel road. More time passed. Then one Saturday afternoon the work of hauling the coal began. Every male in the village assisted. Dorothy's father supervised. Some of the older men helped for short periods; the younger men and many of the schoolboys worked steadily. A few young fellows made some display of effort and then "got lost" in the village, but in three hours twenty tons of coal were carried up the steep incline and dumped into the coal bin. It was the most concerted effort the villagers made during the entire year.

For both parties the adults organized the children's games, secured records for social dancing, and arranged the refreshments for the evening. Participation by the children in the games was voluntary, and so was listening to the instructions on how to play each game. Only those who played and who understood had any chance of winning a prize. The prizes themselves (boxes of Cracker Jack, pocket games) were highly sought.

The highlight of the evening Christmas party at the school was the arrival of Santa Claus, complete in a Santa Claus costume owned by the band, and his distribution of gifts. The children observed some familiar qualities about Santa, his limp, his voice, and the fact that the light was bad so he asked for help to read the name tags; all but the youngest children recognized that more light would not have helped Santa with his inability to read. Girls wore their nicest dresses to the party; most boys wore white shirts and clean jeans and their hair was literally plastered to their heads with water. The children looked and acted their best and the party was a happy occasion.

A tradition of having the children carol through the village on Christmas Eve and receive handouts of cookies was referred to, but on this particular Christmas Eve no caroling occurred. Christmas Day is celebrated as a special occasion in most families and may include a turkey dinner as well as gift-giving. As a time of celebration the occasion can include partying; drinking often preempts other activities. Here is how Dorothy described her Christmas:

> I stayed here during the two week Christmas holiday. But still it was fun. On Christmas Eve Reggie's grandfather and grandmother invited my father and mother for a drinking party over their house. My mother bought some wine for my dad for Christmas.
>
> I got two bobbysocks from Joyce and a 127 film. My brother got me a perfume. From my mother I got a gold belt and a handbag. From Mrs. Alfred George I got a white comb and a bobbypin.
>
> But on Christmas Eve after my mother came home she brought Mr. and Mrs. Gordon Paul to our house for a drinking party. Mrs. Paul was the one who put the fruit in the socks. After they went home I was still awake then. That's when Gordon Paul went out and started fighting with Larry Duncan. Because Larry was fighting with Ed Martin. On Christmas dinner we had a "hangover turkey" those guys called it.

She explained that the "hangover turkey" was named because it was cooked late on Christmas Day. With all the partying, no one had remembered to put the turkey in the oven.

From Christmas through the following summer two more band meetings were held. Both meetings were called by the agent for the purpose of electing council members. Because they were daytime meetings held on school days, the teacher asked permission of the chief councillor and Indian agent to let the older children attend the meetings. At both meetings the children witnessed a formal, agent-dominated session in which the only overt behavior exhibited by most adults was sitting quietly, making no spoken remark during the meeting, and staring out the window or at the floor anytime there was a suggestion that some action, such as a nomination, was essential to the progress of the meeting.

Villagers frequently voiced dissatisfaction with the council system. One problem stems from attempting to impose so formal an organizational structure on a group as small as the Blackfish Band. An extreme example of this was the presence of a locked ballot box which the agent provided (although it was not used) for a village election at which only twelve eligible voters were present. More crucial is the fact that both the authority and the tradition for a chief and council system are administrative devices introduced by the White man; they have no precedent in pre-White culture (Hawthorn *et al.* 1960:35). To elect three men who can sign a release permitting the purchase of fuel for the village water pump is one thing; to elect three men who can "boss everyone around" is quite another.

Reggie's grandfather, the elected chief, complained that while villagers never listened to him ("You might as well be talkin' to a rock") he was held accountable for village behavior by all White officials and even by some older villagers. He complained that villagers did not realize how much he did for the village. Although he has always maintained a good working relationship with the Indian agents, he was frustrated by what he felt was a lack of cooperation in helping the village get a new power plant. He constantly voiced his disapproval of village life and of the way some village families lived, and he spoke often of relinquishing the frustrating position as chief and moving away. When the agent arrived to conduct the election meeting, Reggie's grandfather startled everyone by declining the nomination for reelection.

Villagers who were critical of his leadership were also critical of his refusal to accept the chief's role again; they were so used to having him as chief that they had not considered a successor. No one would accept the nomination although the meeting lasted two hours. The agent finally succeeded in getting a council elected without naming a chief. After the meeting villagers expressed their dissatisfaction with its outcome. For reasons that were never made explicit "Ottawa" did not accept the results of the election and the agent had to call another meeting. In the interim Reggie's grandfather decided that he would accept the nomination "if the people wanted him." He was encouraged by comments made by villagers that he should continue as chief.

After what was for him a long and exasperating meeting at the first election, the agent wanted to assure the success of a second meeting. In the first meeting he had insisted on strict adherence to parliamentary procedure; in the second meeting he encouraged any discussion at all, in English or Kwakwala. He made no demands about the order of nominations. At the start of the meeting he announced that he had been talking with the former chief and the chief had expressed his willingness to run. In a matter of moments the voters present nominated their former chief. When another villager moved to close the nominations the agent declared Reggie's grandfather elected by acclamation. The agent complimented the villagers on the "nice meeting."

In spite of the official sanction for their position and of the formality by which they are selected, councillors are not expected to tell others what they can and cannot do. The older children were disgruntled on the one occasion when the three councillors visited the classroom to lecture about staying out of trouble and staying away from the boats. The only other formal action the councillors took during the year was to post the notice about spring clean up. The attitude of adults toward the council was critical almost as a matter of principle. One woman explained that since she neither went to the election meetings nor voted for anyone, she did not have to do as the councillors directed.

SOCIAL CONTROL

The indigenous and informal means of social control effective within the village do not ignore either the formal organization of the band council or the external sources of control like the RCMP. Villagers did confer with the chief councillor, particularly to complain about other villagers. Threats to "tell the chief" rolled as easily off some tongues as threats to "tell the agent" or to "call the cops" even in intrafamily squabbles. Such threats are usually, although not always, idle ones.

Gossip, subtler and less dramatic than a spoken threat, is a more pervasive and more important mechanism of social control among villagers. Gossip is the consequence of misbehavior, and uneasiness and worry are the consequences of gossip. On several occasions adults and children confided distress over gossip. A villager told me he was seriously considering moving his family away for a while because "some things happened at Christmas and there's been a lot of gossip." Getting out of a bad or uncomfortable situation is an alternative villagers always consider (their stoicism is reserved for unavoidable situations, not for all situations) and an aura of gossip can be a very bad situation. Although I have not been able to assess the dynamics of the role that old women play in village life, I believe they exert much of their influence through gossip control.

The concept of "hearing talk" and the effectiveness of talk as a source of retaliation against wrong-doing is circumscribed and reinforced by folklore, beliefs, and daily behavior. For example, a traditional practice following a death is to burn the clothing and personal possessions of the deceased. This practice is still followed in some households. A failure to observe this custom is believed to detain the departure of the deceased to "the next place they are going," and at night it is said one can hear the voices of the dead if their personal things have been left behind them. Another set of beliefs about the power of talk surrounds the respected blackfish or killer whale. These animals are never to be harmed. If they are harmed, the blackfish "never forget who did it;" at night they come up on the beaches, build huge fires, and talk all evening about their malefactors. At least one villager has heard them talking. No one wishes to be the subject of the talk of the dead, or of the blackfish, or of other villagers.

The positive sanction which complements the negative one of gossip is the extent to which each individual accepts and strives to emulate the behavior expected of a good man, the kind of person for whom other villagers have what they term "respect." Again indigenous and informal values and sanctions serve villagers better than the formal band organization. It is not unknown for a person recently or newly elected to a band council to become overbearing by setting a righteous example and insisting that fellow villagers follow this example. To engage in such behavior for the ultimate purpose of directing (bossing) others is unacceptable behavior which, like any unacceptable behavior, is subject to gossip-control. As long as he does not try to impose his goodness on others, however, a villager is more likely to be considered a good person, worthy of respect, as his behavior exhibits certain qualities. These qualities include being quiet mannered and soft spoken, being generous (in contrast to being stingy), not causing trouble for others, and tending to one's own affairs. To the degree that his behavior approaches these norms a man may expect that his family and friends will respect him, he will be welcome anywhere, no one will walk away from him or lock a door when he comes to visit, and his actions will give no cause for gossip.

PART TWO | The Village School

Village children accept going to school as part of childhood. Most parents attended school and no adult questions the idea that children will attend. Part Two deals with the village school and with the formal education of villagers from a variety of perspectives. An introductory section, "The Educational Setting," traces the start of formal education first at Alert Bay and then at the village. The section includes a description of present-day Canadian Indian education, particularly as it operates within the Kwawkewlth Agency. A second section, "Parents and Teachers," deals with the attitudes and experiences of village adults toward their own and their children's education, with the attitudes and experiences of White teachers in local Indian schools, and with the interaction between parents and teachers. A third section, "The Pupils and the Classroom," describes the attitudes and performance of village children in school. Part Two concludes with a discussion of the education of village children since the period of the study.

4 / The educational setting

THE RESIDENTIAL SCHOOL AT ALERT BAY

THE FIRST MISSION at Alert Bay was established in 1881 under the auspices of the Church of England. A school was started in a room in the mission. Ten years later a separate school building was built. An industrial school and a girl's home were completed next. The large three-story brick St. Michael's Residential School which still dominates the northern end of the reserve at Alert Bay was built in 1929. As school facilities expanded, children were brought in from outlying villages to live at the residence at Alert Bay and to attend school there. Initially the school and the residence were administered as one unit, staffed and operated by the Anglican Church of Canada. Today the instructional program is administered directly by the Indian Affairs Branch in a separate school building and with a separate teaching staff. St. Michael's continues to be operated by the Anglican Church but it is supported partly by government funds and the operation is supervised by the Indian Affairs Branch.

Indian pupils do not pay a fee for staying at St. Michael's. The children who live there are from villages within the Kwawkewlth Agency and from other agencies along the coast. During the 1962–1963 school year two girls from Blackfish Village lived at St. Michael's and attended grade seven at the nearby Indian Day School. Living at St. Michael's and attending the day school is still referred to as "going to St. Mike's." Each year at least two or three children from Blackfish Village attend St. Michael's. Nearly every village parent spent some time there in his youth. Older adults who received any formal education acquired it under Anglican tutelage at Alert Bay. Only two young wives living at the village during the study had attended schools other than at the village or at Alert Bay. These women, the two villagers who have completed the highest education, each attended school through grade eleven. Neither woman is originally from the village.

In its eighty-plus years of operation, the school at Alert Bay has come to occupy a very accepted place in local Indian life. The attitude of children and adults at Blackfish Village toward St. Michael's today is essentially favorable. Everyone can recount stories of good times there, and even recollections concerning discipline are recited with nostalgia, often with a hint that the punishment—usually a loss of privileges—was not inappropriate for the offense. The favorable attitude toward that school results in conflicting attitudes about maintaining a school at the village.

68

Older villagers compare the limited facilities of the village school with their recollections of the program at St. Michael's. They seem oblivious to the fact that many of the features that once made life at the residence so full are no longer part of its activities. A villager who completed grade nine at St. Mike's recalled his full and active schedule when he was a student: participating in intramural sports with games every evening; going to an hour of church service every evening; helping with the school orchard, vegetable gardens, poultry, and dairy; learning to drive farm tractors and trucks; receiving manual training in such activities as looking after the boilers, taking care of machinery, and totem pole carving; going to classes in boat-building and navigation; singing and presenting concerts; and taking turns at helping in the work of the laundry, kitchen, woodshed, farm, bakery, and cleaning the grounds. "There were no holidays like kids have now," he reflected; "there wasn't an idle moment." For discipline, "If something went wrong, everyone had to stay in and work all weekend if no one owned up." The program included the weekly showing of a film, a tradition that is still a popular recruiting device for children reluctant to leave their families and go away to school.

Life at St. Michael's today holds less variety. Since the school and residence are separate, all teaching except for religious instruction is conducted by a faculty completely removed from the staff and program of St. Michael's. Time at the residence is filled with homework, housekeeping chores, sports, and television. Recent administrative changes have resulted in considerable staff turnover. There have been mumblings among Alert Bay residents about the constant changes and the supervision of pupils. Such changes and problems are far from the view of the villagers who hold, in almost total agreement, that little can happen at the residence that is any worse or more difficult than life at the village. To villagers the bigger school, with its better facilities and constant supervision and care, is far superior. One villager summed up the feeling of many parents when he told the superintendent of Indian schools that he believes that residential school is the "best kind," a place where "kids really learn." He stated, "If I had the chance, I would send the children there tomorrow." He complained to the superintendent about village parents who drink constantly and who "won't even buy food for their children." His recommendation was that all the children in his village should be sent off to the residential school because at Blackfish Village "too few can take care of their own." A former villager expressed his skepticism of any educational program operating at the village: "How can you change the children when they go right back to their houses each day?"

Official Branch policy during the time of this study was that Indian parents should be responsible for their own children and rightfully should have their children live at home just as White parents do; consequently, schools should be maintained on the reserve if provincial schools are not accessible. Some officials feel that while Indian parents want residential school for *other* Indian children, they prefer to keep their own children at home. The latter sentiment does not hold among Blackfish Village parents. While villagers stated that the only way to handle "those bad boys" (some of the older school-age boys) was to send them to St. Michael's, they stated a preference for having their own children attend school there as well.

Former villagers who now reside at Alert Bay always mention the problem of getting a good education for their children as one of the reasons they left the village. One group of parents who left Blackfish Village intended their move to Alert Bay to be only temporary until their children completed school. They were ultimately confronted by the Indian agent with the alternatives of either transferring their official band membership to Alert Bay or returning to Blackfish Village. There was no school at the village at that particular time. They chose to remain at the bay. Villagers who have moved away have, in fact, secured more education for their children, have higher educational aspirations for them, and have encouraged them to stay in school longer.

Parents who commented on the inadequacy of the village school were not critical of its academic program as much as they regretted the lack of opportunity for washing before meals, saying grace, observing table manners, keeping well groomed, and having an opportunity for organized team games and a continually supervised program. Young parents also feel that it is better for children not to "hear Indian talk all the time." English is the lingua franca at St. Michael's since most of the staff are White and since the range of dialects of the children from more distant villages includes dialects that are not mutually comprehensible. Children say they are warned not to use their native language in front of supervisors and are threatened with punishment if they do so.

Except for the reluctance some parents showed toward sending their children to Alert Bay in the early days of the school, the residential school has always been filled and has generally had a waiting list. The residence has accommodated up to 200 children and has provided both living quarters and classroom facilities within the one building. The Branch today limits the number of children in residence to about 150. Many parents in outlying villages who would prefer to send their children to Alert Bay to school cannot do so because of the limited number of places available. Indeed, the only consistent criticism of the operation of the residential school by villagers is the policy of bringing children from distant areas since this deprives their own children of the opportunity to attend. The intensity of this feeling was evident in December 1962 when three fifteen-year-old Indian boys drowned while attempting to row from Alert Bay to a neighboring island. What had motivated such a trip and whether the boys had been drinking were never clearly established. The boys were reported to have tried earlier that fall to enroll in St. Michael's, but they were not accepted because the residence was full. The boys had nothing to do during the fall. The reaction to the drowning was: "If St. Mike's wasn't filled up by the kids from the north, those three boys would still be alive today."

HISTORY OF FORMAL EDUCATION AT BLACKFISH VILLAGE

Until 1928 any formal education received by village children necessitated attendance at a residential school. In that year, at the same time that the present St. Michael's was being completed, an Englishwoman by the name of Miss Kathleen O'Brien and a companion, Miss M. E. Nixon, arrived at Blackfish Village to establish a school, regular religious services and medical care. Miss O'Brien was a nurse. She had spent the three preceding years at Alert Bay in public health work among the Indian population. She saw a need for intermediate medical care for cases that did not require hospitalization in the crowded government hospital but that required more constant attention than she felt could be counted on in most Indian homes. When she met with resistance to the idea of establishing a nursing facility at Alert Bay, she decided to go to an outlying village instead. At the time of her arrival at Blackfish Village the community had ninety-five members. She remained in the village for twenty-two years, leaving at the age of seventy to return to England. For her work she was awarded the "Member of the British Empire" by King George VI, an occasion to which she referred modestly in a personal communication as "a *King's Honour* out of the Blue." In her honor villagers have placed a beautifully lettered sign on the village school, "O'Brien Memorial School." The sign is a recognition of how the older villagers felt about her and continue to feel today, although the school is never referred to by her name.

Miss O'Brien and Miss Nixon were the first White people to live in the village. Miss Nixon conducted school and initiated regular religious services; Miss O'Brien offered medical assistance. The church, the government, and their own private funds were the financial sources upon which the women drew, although villagers feel that Miss O'Brien supported most of the work with her own money. A teacherage was built and Miss O'Brien remained to serve as nurse and missionary and to oversee a procession of younger women who taught school after Miss Nixon's departure in 1931. After 1940 the school was not staffed for eleven years, but Miss O'Brien continued her work in the village conducting religious services and operating a tuberculosis solarium or "preventorium." According to villagers it was Miss O'Brien's work in establishing the village preventorium that led eventually to the opening of such units, primarily for tuberculosis patients, elsewhere along the coast. Miss O'Brien reflected on her work in a personal letter as follows:

> Our job was to live a Christian life of kindliness and cleanliness especially with cases of TB all around. The Government had at first no provision for TB cases as now. The very small hospital at Alert Bay could not keep them. I wish I could have been more helpful.

According to Miss O'Brien's recollection only a few people in the village could understand and speak more than a few words of English when she arrived. One or two older children acted as interpreters. She recalled no feeling of hostility toward her or toward Whites in general. Concerning school she wrote, "I think many of the parents felt sure the boys especially needed education to make their way and were glad of schools."

Although she was never directly responsible for the classroom program, it is Miss O'Brien's name that is associated with the start of the school. After her departure people state that "there just wasn't any way to get schooling" in the village, vaguely ascribing to her the power to provide a teacher, yet for the last years of her stay in the village, from 1940 to 1950, no teacher was assigned. The disparity between her own modest report and the glowing recollections of her admirers in the village makes it difficult to assess her impact. Perhaps her influence is best summed up in the comment of one villager who said, "After she was gone, everything going to pieces again."

INDIAN EDUCATION WITHIN THE AGENCY

When school opened in September 1962, an enrollment of 340 pupils was expected in the eight local Indian day schools. Fourteen teachers were on hand to staff these eight schools. Six teachers were assigned to the large day school at Alert Bay, one of whom also acted as principal. At one outlying village there were to be two teachers, and one teacher was assigned to each school in six other villages.

Since the day schools are elementary schools, Indian pupils who go on to high school attend the provincial school at Alert Bay or attend high schools elsewhere in the province. However, no child from Blackfish Village attended high school during 1962–1963 and no native villager had ever attended a provincial school.

Until after World War II, Indian agents administered the local education programs. The Indian agent is still in charge of the physical plant at each day school. Janitorial supplies and routine maintenance are handled through his office. Since he is the most readily available official of the Indian Affairs Branch, and since he is conversant with most local problems, the agent also influences other aspects of the operation of the schools, such as teacher accommodations and local problems as they arise for individual teachers. One agent commented, not completely facetiously, that his problems were about equally divided between the 2500 Indians and the fourteen teachers within his jurisdiction.

The hiring of teachers and the organization of the instructional program are carried out under the direction of the regional superintendent of Indian schools of the province through a district superintendent in Nanaimo. The regional superintendent, and superintendents from other provinces, are ultimately responsible to the assistant deputy minister of the Indian Affairs Branch in Ottawa. The legal authority for providing education for Indian children is provided in the Indian Act.

Teacher recruitment for Indian schools has always been a nagging or, as one official described it, a "wearisome" problem. The problem is aggravated by the pressure of competitive provincial salary schedules and by the continual increase in the number of Indian children in school. The regional superintendent posed the dilemma: Which is better—to open every school every year, even if it means staffing it with little more than a warm body, or to close schools when competent teachers are not available?

Annual teacher turnover is staggering. Among the 238 teachers in the Indian schools administered by the regional superintendent in Vancouver there was a turnover of ninety teachers in the summer of 1962. Only twenty of the teachers hired as replacements were interviewed prior to hiring. Within the Kwawkewlth Agency's roster of fourteen teachers, five were new in the 1962–1963 school year. During the year one replacement had to be found. At the close of school the following June, eleven of the fourteen positions were vacant again.

On paper the salaries and qualifications for teachers in Indian schools are not generally different from those of the provincial schools. In fact, however, teachers qualified to teach in the provincial schools do not typically apply for teaching positions with the Indian Affairs Branch. As a group, the teachers in Indian schools are less well qualified by training or experience, and general impressions of them which visitors carry away are characteristically unfavorable. One observer noted:

> The school teachers I met were rather uniformly badly trained, limited and prejudiced people. The most frequent type was the middle-aged English woman whose goals were as stingily personal as could be imagined.

The salary schedule for Branch schools makes finer distinctions among factors that are prequalifying for full certification. Whether it is true or not, a teacher who was concluding four years of teaching in a nearby village believed that his time spent teaching in an Indian school would not be accepted as teaching experience by the provincial schools in determining his place on the salary schedule.

Salaries, conditions, and minimum qualifications improve continually but slowly. During the year of the study teachers in Indian schools received a retroactive pay raise based on a salary schedule adopted in May 1963. The schedule ranged from $2200 to $2700 for unqualified and inexperienced teachers, from $2900 to $5600 for qualified teachers with no experience, and to a maximum salary of $8600. Teachers at Indian schools also receive a monthly isolation allowance determined by the location of the school and the number of dependents. This enables the Branch to offer teachers more than the stated salary, and it provides an incentive for accepting positions in the outlying schools where the allowances are higher. At Blackfish Village the allowance equalled the monthly rent.

In May 1963, a news bulletin announced a program enabling teachers from provincial schools to teach for one year in Indian schools at their current salary. The Branch was eager to accept any teachers who were interested in a year of such service. As usual, many positions were still unfilled as the next school year approached. The superintendent confided with real despair:

> Teacher recruitment has been most difficult. I suppose this area should naturally have received top priority but I am not sure that anything that we are able to do will help the situation appreciably.

Canadian education is constitutionally a provincial matter. Although Indian education is the ultimate responsibility of the federal government, federal policy attempts to provide the Indian child with school facilities and opportunities comparable to those of the province. In general the school calendar, the school curriculum, and the textbooks for the province are used in Indian schools within that province.

Schools in British Columbia are open almost ten months, from early in September until the end of June. The 1962–1963 school year was 197 days. Provincial schools do not have kindergartens. Students enroll in grade one at the age of six years or if they will be six during the calendar year. Students attending provincial schools must purchase their own books and supplies, but supplies are issued free to pupils in Indian schools.

In the educational system of the Branch, the regional superintendent holds a cen-

tral position in the operation of the Indian schools within the province. The operation of each school is theoretically under two administrative units, the department
of education of the province and the regional superintendent of Indian Schools.
District superintendents of the provincial schools are considered welcome and
official guests when they visit (or, in Canada, "inspect") Indian schools. This dual
administration of the schools poses problems for Indian education. Special materials are not developed for Indian education, yet there are many situations in which
special materials would be more appropriate for Indian children. Because requisi-
tions for supplies are based on the official grade-level attendance reports, teachers
in Indian schools may be denied materials which they feel are appropriate because
the students are officially reported in higher grades. One inspector is said to have
instructed a village teacher to use only texts of the grade level to which the students
were officially assigned, a policy that would be a sure recipe for failure. Similarly,
the provincial school calendar does not take into account local social or subsistence
activities of importance and there are no provisions for releasing pupils at such
times. In short, the Indian schools operate with an official curriculum which sets
the same course and uses the same materials as that of the provincial schools, a cen-
tralized program that lacks sensitivity to local problems but brings some satisfaction
because it is the same everywhere.

School inspections at Blackfish Village during the year included several visits by
the Indian agent, a brief introductory visit and one official inspection later in the
year by the district superintendent, no visit by provincial officers, a brief visit by the
Indian commissioner (his first to the village), and visits by the regional superintendent which included time for talking to many villagers and for meeting with the
chief councillor. Such a visiting schedule for the year represented a far greater
number of official visitors than had come to the village in the past, reflecting a
combination of more vigorous interest in Indian education, an increased dedication
among new appointees to administrative postions, and specific interest in the present study.

THE BLACKFISH INDIAN DAY SCHOOL

During Miss O'Brien's first two years at Blackfish Village, school was held intermittently. After September 1930, a teacher was assigned regularly every school year
until June 1940. From 1940 until April 1951, no outside teacher was appointed.
No one seems to recall just why no teacher was sent, although the band had remained small, increasing from ninety-five in 1929 to only 107 in 1939. The national teacher shortage during and immediately after World War II is given as the
official reason why no teacher was available. Several families moved away from the
village during this period when there was no teacher, and although they felt that
their move to Alert Bay was temporary, none of the families ever returned. Parents
who remained at the village could still send their children to St. Michael's, if there
was room. But more children were being brought to the residence from along the
coast and the waiting list continued to grow.

Had it been possible for villagers to continue enrolling their children at St. Michael's, it is unlikely there would ever have been much interest in starting a school

at the village again. To Reggie's grandfather, a staunch supporter of education and a spokesman among villagers in this regard, the "last straw" to the problem of getting an education for his own children came when he returned to the village one day during the fall fishing to find his two youngest children back in the village after he had enrolled them at the residence. The children had been sent home, he was told, because there were not enough places at St. Michael's and his children "lived the closest." Under such circumstances villagers felt that they would be better off with a school at the village. They made their wishes known to the commissioner of the Indian Affairs Branch in Vancouver and were promised that a new school would be built and staffed at Blackfish Village.

In April 1951, a woman teacher arrived at the village to start school again. She remained only four months, but the teacher position had been officially reactivated, and the following summer a new young teacher arrived with his wife and family. He was the first male teacher at the village school. He and his family lived in one of the homes that had formerly belonged to an Indian resident, and he conducted school in another small house in the center of the village until the present building, a two-classroom school and teacherage, was completed.

During the two-year stay of the next teacher, enrollment warranted operating both classrooms. Since the teacher's wife did not wish to teach, a woman who came in as the second teacher had to share the teacherage. From January 1955 until June 1959 the second classroom was used, with the second class conducted most often by the wife of the teacher. No teacher for the second classroom was appointed after 1959.

The school building has two large classrooms, an inner hall and stairway leading to the basement, and toilets and washrooms for boys and girls. In the same building is a teacherage with three bedrooms, a bathroom, a living room, and a large kitchen. Basement facilities include two large rooms plus a furnace room and coal bin. In 1962 the building was piped for propane gas and a new propane kitchen stove and hot water heater were installed. The school has its own diesel-powered electric generator.

In some ways the design of the school plant illustrates the problem of imposing bureaucratic standards from as far away as Ottawa. Installation of a coal furnace to heat the teacherage has caused the recurring problem of finding a means of transporting a yearly shipment of coal from the wharf up to the school. Another problem concerns water use at the school. The Branch has spent years futilely trying to develop a dependable water source for the village. Yet the school is equipped with five flush toilets and a flush urinal. From past teacher notes and my own experience, I suspect that there have always been several dry weeks at the school when the only water available has been carried in buckets from the nearest tap down in the village. Since all the local island villages are plagued with water shortages the heavy water use in schools and teacherages creates ill feeling during these critical times. In one village the chief councillor personally turned off the water line to a urinal and instructed the teacher that it was not to be turned on again.

During the year the Civil Service Association of Canada completed a survey among teachers at Indian schools throughout British Columbia and distributed copies of its findings and recommendations. The report identified three major problems for all Indian day schools: *isolation, substandard housing,* and *inadequate repair and maintenance.* All three problems have been of major concern in the operation of the Blackfish Indian Day School. The problems are elaborated here because of their effect on teachers and ultimately on the pupils and the community. Each problem takes a share of a teacher's enthusiasm and energy.

The first problem, isolation, is recognized as inevitable. The report recommends that attempts should be made to reduce periods of complete isolation. The report recognizes that teachers typically become very dependent on the Indian community for supplies, mail, and social life, and that "if, for any reason, friction develops between the teacher and the villagers, then life for the teacher can be made completely miserable."

The report recommends more frequent visits by department officials, suggesting that such visits tend to reduce isolation and provide an opportunity for an outsider to smooth out sources of friction between teacher and community. The report observes that "the problems arising in isolation tend to grow out of all proportion to their actual size and importance." Not one local day school teacher escaped getting caught up in problems which needed at least the sympathetic ear of an outsider and usually needed some direct action. Before more frequent visits will become an answer, however, there may have to be changes both in their traditionally "inspecting" nature and in their duration. Most official visits to village schools are made while a chartered plane waits at the float.

The geographical isolation complicates ordering and obtaining materials for the classroom as well as for the teacher's own needs. A previous village teacher had recorded these comments about supplies:

> Our wood for the year we received in March, our coal by mistake (should have gone to Dead Point), the school supplies some in November, some in February and the better part in May.

In a context broader than only the geographic one, isolation was identified as the "cardinal factor" in the problem of formal Indian education in another modern-day Indian community (Wax *et al.* 1964:102). The authors of that study consider the social aspects of isolation as well as geographical ones. All the contexts of isolation which they found contributing to the problems of teachers at an Indian residential school affect village teachers: isolation of the Indian community from the mainstream of modern life, isolation of teachers from Indian parents, isolation within the classroom resulting from mutual rejection between teacher and pupils, and the isolation of teachers at Indian schools both from other teachers and from their own metropolitan society.

The second problem identified in the civil service survey, substandard housing, concerns not only what the report termed "woefully inferior" housing but also some apparently widespread complaints about leaking roofs, improper drainage, inadequate water supplies, and the high rents charged to teachers for accommodations. The rent of $70 per month, utilities included, for a clean and comfortably furnished house did not seem unreasonable for the large teacherage at Blackfish Village.

Repairs and maintenance are part of the problem of substandard housing, but for emphasis they were given separate attention in the civil service survey. Blackfish villagers discussed how former teachers have faced perennial problems not only with the water supply but also with fuel, with the power plant, and with the old kitchen stove. A predecessor in the teacherage wrote this account of the school as he found it:

> To say that the building was filthy and without water hard to get clean is conservative. On arrival it stank. After a while fellow teachers in Alert Bay could smell the odour on my jacket. . . . The toilets were unapproachable and it took one of the strongest young men in the village as much courage as he could muster to go in for an hour a day and attempt to clean them. Only a broken corn broom was available to clean with at first. The bedroom chests had store string handles on them and somewhat new furniture was thick with grease and dust. The flooring was thick with grime the teacherage really unlivable. We found thick soap leavings in the soup ladle. . . . Nothing worked on arrival. The Diesel Plant which supplies the school with lights had two cracked batteries to start it. . . . Basement Furnaces were plugged on arrival and the whole year the water heater (cracked) was really useless. Our hot water we heated on the stove. Periodically the classroom furnaces which were plugged and unusable on arrival would blow up and the classrooms, full of smoke were in extreme danger of fire many times. Similarly the Kitchen stove would blow back.

The teacher who wrote this account was overwhelmed by both the physical plant and by his Indian pupils. He opened school for four days in September, then closed it for twenty days while he worked sporadically at maintenance tasks until he finally retreated back to Alert Bay. After a rainfall he returned to the village but still there was no running water. His lack of experience and commitment to teaching might have prevented his success, but he was already beaten by the school plant. Although his long report may have been responsible for the many improvements that were made at the school after his departure, there was little sympathy toward the man expressed by either villagers or Indian Affairs Branch officials.

Prior to 1962 only minimal attention had been given to maintenance at schools within the agency. The backlog of needed work was gigantic, and one crew worked most of the year at the eight schools. Providing lodging for work crews is a problem except during the summer when teachers are away. Crew members spent over three months lodged in the teacherage at Blackfish Village during the school year 1962–1963 although the teacher was paying rent on the house as his own. Generally the arrival of the maintenance crew had an excellent effect on teacher morale at all the schools within the agency.

Even routine custodial tasks like sweeping classrooms and cleaning lavatories may become problems at village schools. Some local teachers perform their own custodial services, not so much for the small stipend allowed but because of the difficulty of obtaining a dependable villager who will do the work. The teachers who do their own janitorial work may feel some reluctance in giving pupils too easy access to all school facilities, particularly the lavatories. Conversely, teachers who employ a villager as janitor occasionally find that a lack of agreement about the time or standards for cleaning the school create serious friction between the school and at least one village household.

5 / Parents and teachers

THE EDUCATIONAL ACHIEVEMENT OF VILLAGE ADULTS

IT IS NOT POSSIBLE to give a precise picture of the educational achievement of village adults. Grade levels in the day school today, as in the past, have little meaning except to indicate a relative standing among pupils. Adults are not always sure what grade they attained: "We were in grade eight doing correspondence, but I think it was really grade four work." Sickness and local migrations have interrupted attendance and often teachers did not know what grade level to assign to their pupils. There frequently was some disparity between what villagers stated as their highest grade attained and what others said they attained or what school records showed. Some adults received tutorial help during periods of hospitalization which helped them make great strides in skills of literacy although their formal education was limited to only one or two grades. For example, after one woman attended two years of school at St. Michael's she developed an illness that required years of medical care. She reported that she spent five years in the preventorium, and that "We had a nurse and a teacher and we did about two hours of school each day." When she returned to St. Michael's she was assigned to, but did not complete, grade five.

Table I shows the highest grade attained by village adults. Information is based on what individuals reported for themselves or for others and by reference to school records. The median average grade attainment is given for different age groups. Generally younger siblings have continued their education for as long or longer than older siblings, and with only one exception each generation within a family has attended school longer than the generation preceding it. In the latter case the father blames the crowded conditions at St. Michael's for the fact that his children did not attend school there as long as he did.

While young people are staying in school longer, it is apparent from Table 1 that their total grade attainment still falls short of opening up opportunities that have formal education as a prerequisite. Villagers are aware that children in other villages have tended to stay in school longer and that some have gone on to high school. Reggie's grandfather commented, "I guess we are the lowest in education around here."

Many neighboring villagers have the impression that children at Blackfish Village are particularly slow and reluctant in school. They offer a variety of explanations: children in the other villages speak more English, Blackfish children have no respect for authority, and they have always had a reputation for disliking school

TABLE 1

HIGHEST GRADE ATTAINED OR COMPLETED BY BLACKFISH VILLAGE ADULTS
(1962)

		Number of Adults Attaining Each Grade Level												Number of Adults in Age Group	Median Grade Achievement for Age Group
Present Age	No School	1	2	3	4	5	6	7	8	9	10	11		
15–24	0	0	0	0	1	3	5	7	2	0	0	1	19	7
25–34	2	0	0	4	1	1	0	2	0	0	0	1	11	3
35–44	2	0	0	0	1	1	1	0	2	1	0	0	8	5.5
45–54	1	0	0	0	1	1	0	0	0	0	0	0	3	4
55–64	3	0	1	1	0	0	0	0	0	0	0	0	5	0
65–74	1	0	0	0	0	0	0	0	0	0	0	0	1	0
75–84	1	0	0	0	0	0	0	0	0	0	0	0	1	0
Adults Attaining Each Grade	10	0	1	5	4	6	6	9	4	1	0	2	48	

and quitting early. The precedent for attending beyond grade school has never been established in the village, while in a few neighboring villages there is a longer history of village schooling and children have received encouragement from teachers or missionaries to continue their formal education.

ATTITUDES TOWARD EDUCATION

Expressed vaguely as a desirable something to have, education is highly endorsed by villagers. A sixteen-year-old from a neighboring village epitomized the feeling with the declaration, "I think education is the *only* answer." Considering the boy's school record, even this stereotyped remark seems a remarkable vote of confidence for the schools. For his ten years of schooling the records contained only one subjective entry about him ("Sly, torments smaller children, lies, cheats, and needs a firm hand") and showed the following progress:

Grade I	"C" average
Grade II	"C+" average
Grade III	did it twice
Grade IV	did it twice
Grade V	did it twice
Grade VI	"C+" average
Grade VII	"C−" average

Yet this boy looked forward to entering a grade eight class at Alert Bay and hoped to "do grade ten at least." His aspirations were similar to those expressed by several village youths. The actual circumstances at the termination of his schooling are also typical. He was expelled from school the following year as a troublemaker. At the beginning of the next school year he was serving a sentence for repeated liquor violations. At the next opening of school, as an 18-year-old, he did not even consider returning to an eighth-grade classroom.

Pupils within the classroom express the prevailing platitudes of the necessity for school. They admonish fellow pupils for poor attendance with such comments as, "How you gonna smarten up if you don't go to school?" or warnings that if one does not go to school he will be "*really* dumb."

Parents talk of "pushing" their children, particularly the young ones, to go far in school. The push, if it comes at all, is tacit rather than coercive. The decision of how far a child will go in school is left to the child himself. Most parents remain noncommital in their aspirations for their children except for vague educational goals like "as far as he can go" or "all the way." Yet the pride of literacy among the old people reinforces a precedent for acquiring literacy, and it is assumed that children will learn to read and write. Such a goal is not unreasonable as the one major expectation from ten required years of schooling. Abilities in reading and writing, basic computational skills, and an acquisition of an assortment of historical and geographical facts are referred to globally by villagers as "that stuff you learn in school."

Differentiations among parental aspirations for their children seem related to the extent of their own formal education. The aspirations of one villager who never attended school (his father would not allow it) are that his boys maintain a level of school attendance adequate to keep welfare and Family Allowance benefits coming regularly. While he is not adverse to having his children learn to read and write, he does not insist upon it. Walter's father, who had attended through "senior fourth" at St. Michael's wants his children to "write and read," skills which he did not completely master. Reggie's parents, both educated through grade seven, hope their children will graduate from high school. Dorothy's father, with a grade eight education, is proud to explain that his daughter sometimes says she "might like to be a nurse or teacher." Norma, the oldest of the school pupils, had already exceeded the education attained by any of her older siblings. No one in her household was particularly concerned about how much longer she would remain in school.

While education is often spoken of as a panacea among those villagers with little or no schooling, on occasion formal education is used as a rebuke against people who have been to school. A boy from another village back from high school for summer fishing was criticized by fellow fishermen for his lack of skill as a crewman, especially because he had "all that education." The comment was made within the village about one woman: "She has a good education, but look at her. She can't do anything." Several boys within the local area had completed high school and had returned to find themselves out of the mainstream of local life, neither adequately prepared for a new vocation nor satisfied with maintaining a village way of life. Aware of the training they can receive, they comfort themselves with talk of the possibility of returning to school. Practically speaking, their educational attainment has opened no doors through which they choose to pass. Yet only once during the year did I hear anyone state that schooling alone cannot guarantee "the answer." "Education isn't the whole thing," cautioned this native in a talk to members of the Native Brotherhood. "It also takes courage."

WHAT VILLAGERS EXPECT OF A TEACHER

Through their own experiences in school and their experiences with teachers at the village, the adults have come to expect certain kinds of behavior from a teacher. These expectations have considerable impact on the nature of the teacher-community interaction, for they are the shared expectations of the village community. The teacher, too, holds expectations about how teachers should act and how others should act toward him. The sources of his experiences, however, are rooted in the traditions of the dominant society rather than in village life. There is potential conflict when expectations from the two sources are not compatible. When such conflicts occur, it is the teacher whose expectations diverge from group consensus within the village. The lack of shared expectations is a crucial factor in producing conflict both between the teacher and his pupils and between the teacher and villagers in general.

The teacher is expected to be "smart" about the teaching of reading and writing —that domain is left almost exclusively to him. Teachers are also perceived as a sort of repository of facts: "Ask him, he's the teacher." When the teacher does not have the answer surprise is usually registered. This expectation contrasts with the behavior of villagers, most of whom show little interest in commanding facts and minimize any evidence of controlling information, especially to an outsider. A frequently heard response to any inquiry is, "I just wouldn't know."

The teacher is expected to know how to run a school and to be able to run it "the right way" as measured primarily by three criteria: opening school every day, starting it on time, and keeping pupils busy. When villagers judge that the teacher is running a good school, based on these criteria, they refer to him as a "good teacher."

The credentials of the teachers who come to the village are not of much concern to villagers. They assume that their teachers are not sufficiently qualified to do more than "teach Indians." However, a story is told that in one village the councillors begged the superintendent to send them, at least once, a teacher who said "with" instead of "mit." There are a number of non-Canadians engaged in both Indian education and Indian health services, including persons who have difficulty with English.

The community has no voice in the selection of a teacher. The Branch issues a person to them, a stranger who will reside only temporarily in the village, perhaps not even for the entire school year. This transitory aspect of the teacher's presence in the village pervades the teacher-community relationship. Villagers take for granted that the tenure of their assigned stranger will be brief. Reggie's grandfather often expressed his wish that teachers would remain more than a year, although he acknowledged that the village is a "tough place" for a teacher to live. His solution: "You city fellows don't like it here but maybe if they get someone from around these parts who would stay here it would be better."

Even the youngest pupil has already seen a procession of teachers come and go, and every teacher's departure is only a matter of time. To illustrate how transitory teachers appear to children: On the three-day October weekend of Canadian Thanksgiving I left the village for the holiday. By coincidence, a teacher and her husband from another village came by to borrow school supplies just as I was leaving. Although I had explained to the children about my trip, my plane had only taxied from the float when an eight-year-old girl turned to the visitor to inquire, "Are you our new teacher?"

Villagers expect the teacher to be the disciplinarian for other people's children and even for their own children "if they need it." By assigning the responsibility for disciplining to the teacher, villagers set him apart from all other village adults. Past teachers have included some stern disciplinarians. A strap is standard classroom equipment. Dorothy's mother explained how she interpreted the teacher's discipline to her own children: "If he straps you, that's his business." Yet she explained to me that while she recalls the strappings that were given in school, she never spanks her children and she does not believe in it.

During a discussion about school at the first band meeting of the new term there was an exchange in Kwakwala and then the chief councillor turned to me and said, "Mrs. Willie [Walter's mother] wants you to strap the children when they bad." I asked if the people strapped their own children and was told that they did not. The conflicting feelings about discipline show in these comments which another parent made to me a few days after that meeting:

> When Mrs. Willie said in that meeting, "You should beat the kids," why I wanted to say, "But you don't beat them." But I'm too—how do you say—shy, so I don't say anything. She doesn't beat them. But we want our kids to know discipline, and that day when our son was out of school when the Inspector was here my husband hit him with a belt. And I didn't say anything. But it hurt me. And I don't like it.
>
> You can tell which kids have discipline. We want discipline for our kids. I tell our son, "You must never steal."

Whenever behavior problems like sucking gas, bullying, or using slingshots seemed to be getting out of hand, councillors or other adults came directly to me to complain and to instruct me to "do something about it." Older children often expressed overt hostility toward me at such times in anticipation of disciplinary action requested by village adults. "What did he tell you to do to us?" they asked. On one occasion two mothers came to the school to complain of treatment their youngsters were receiving from children in other families. Immediately after their visit Norma wrote:

> Today is Monday and a horrible day, [Mrs.] Alfred and [Mrs.] Willie are complaining of course, they're always complaining about the Duncans Fords and Hawkins. Mrs. Alfred thinks her kids are good, and yet there just as worse as the Duncan boys. Gee. I don't know what to call her. But I'll ask my mother when she comes home.

Past teachers have often been outspoken in their disapproval of many facets of village life. They have scolded and lectured. Villagers have come to expect such behavior from teachers. A neighboring teacher confessed, "I used to have a PTA [Parent-Teacher Association]. When I called a meeting, they would say, 'All right, what are you going to bawl us out for now?'" Parents minimize their being lectured in two ways. First, they keep the teacher from knowing too much about what goes on in the village. Second, they avoid placing themselves in any social position with the teacher which might subject them to his sermonizing about how to behave or what is wrong with their way of doing things. Such avoidance behavior is not limited to teachers; other Whites, such as the agent, the RCMP, and the nurses are often avoided. The same avoidance behavior is manifested toward the councillors and toward any older villagers who might disapprove of behavior. It is more difficult to keep information from fellow villagers, but it is possible to avoid meeting them in the village, to avoid band meetings, and to counter their real or imagined disapproval by gossiping about how "some people" try to run everything or to tell others how to act.

In addition to the generally disparaging attitude toward village life that villagers have come to expect from a teacher, they also suspect that like most other Whites he will believe himself to be superior to Indians. This expectation that the teacher will think he is superior has a compensating element: given the stress of living in the village for any length of time, the day inevitably comes when the teacher exhibits qualities of human fallibility. The teacher's deviance from expected or proper behavior is watched and noted. This became evident to me the first time I joined some villagers for a few beers. Prior to that year liquor had been illegal on the reserve. The children were aware of the covert nature of village drinking in the past, and my participation in the drinking seemed to incur anger, shock, and perhaps disappointment among them. Nevertheless, their reactions suggested some satisfaction as well, for they had caught me doing something they felt was wrong. A similar attitude was revealed more boldly in an incident later in the year. Several people, including some single women, were weekend guests at the teacherage. Partying on boats tied at the float loosened the tongue of one village parent who shouted angrily at the teacherage as she passed it late on Saturday evening, "You fucker, Harry, *You're no better than the rest of us.* We're going to get you —we'll drown you one of these days."

Villagers expect the teacher to have a hard time managing the classroom. "Kids here are pretty used to having their own way," Dorothy's father explained with resignation when I gave a too-candid response about how things were going in school. Near the end of the school year his wife explained to me what she had done that she felt was responsible for the good behavior of her children in class: "I could have told my kids not to listen to you in school, but I never did."

The teacher is expected to be honest and dependable. Such an expectation finds precedence in the emphasis which teachers traditionally give to instruction in moral values like honesty and in the fact that a teacher in an Indian school is a representative of the federal government. Several past teachers have assumed the responsibility for conducting religious services in the village as well. Villagers associate these traits with honesty. Teachers have usually been trusted with loans or credit in spite of at least two experiences in recent years that might have taught villagers differently.

Young adults and older school children like to recall certain privileges and good times allowed by former teachers and they cite them as examples of how nice certain teachers were. Whether by design or not, local villagers often include a discussion of the merits of former teachers in the presence of newcomers. Such comments as "Gee, the ———s were really nice people" may be interpreted by newcomers to mean they do not quite measure up to former teachers in extending hospitality or favors.

Whether the over-all feeling of each villager toward a new teacher is positive or negative reflects both his experience with specific teachers and his generalized attitudes toward all Whites and toward White authority. The range of these feelings is better demonstrated through the unsophisticated behavior of the very young children than in the guarded actions of the adults. During my first few hours at the school, while I was still unpacking, three young children started throwing rocks at the building, expressing their regard for the new occupant of the building before they had ever seen him. When I went outside to see what was happening I was confronted with the first words spoken to me in the village. A little girl warned me of one of her rock-throwing playmates, "Look out, he's going to kick you in the ass." I foolishly ignored the warning. In contrast, there were other preschoolers whose waves and greetings suggested that the teacher was not automatically to be treated as an enemy.

Villagers exhibited a variety of behaviors which suggested the range of their perceptions about me. After attending my first band meeting I was told that the chief councillor had announced in Kwakwala that the village now had "the best teacher we ever had," and that villagers were to help me in every way to "get you things and so on." Villagers did offer help in a variety of ways, particularly with providing transportation and with getting mail and groceries for me. I occasionally received gifts of freshly-baked goods, cooked crabs, and barbecued and canned salmon. Sometimes I was invited to join parties. Adults and children visited at the teacherage in a constant procession.

Some formal distance was maintained by the pupils and by most of the women through addressing me as "Mr. Wolcott" (although reference to me in Kwakwala was always made by the word for White man). Alcohol seemed to intensify either the positive or negative attitude each adult had toward me and to increase the likelihood of his communicating these feelings. During a visit to the teacherage prompted by drinking earlier in the evening, a usually reticent parent was able to confide, "We're all related here, you know. We're all just one big family here. While you're here you're one of us and we love you and that's why we came to see you." By contrast, another parent's negative feelings toward me were released by the effects of alcohol and she shouted at me across the village, "Come here, asshole Wolcott, I'm not going to be sucker for you. Come here, you asshole. I'm going to kill you."

Because during my tenure school ran regularly and on time and because I was not "stupid" (i.e., the children had school work to do), no complaints were voiced directly. Probably the most interesting observation about my acceptance as a teacher was made to me by Reggie's father when he said at the end of the school year, "I think what we need here is a teacher who isn't *too* smart."

COMMUNICATION BETWEEN PARENTS AND THE TEACHER

Several modes of communication exist between parents and the teacher. At one extreme was the treatment accorded me by two of the oldest women—they avoided ever confronting me directly. Some parents avoided interaction with me by limiting conversations to formal greetings or to a brief exchange about the weather. I had the feeling during the year that for short periods of time every adult in the village avoided me. I do not know if this was conscious behavior by villagers, mere coincidence, or a symptom of isolation. Other local teachers reported a similar perception. At least once during the year a parent from every household in the village initiated some kind of conference concerning children in school. The time and place of these visits varied enough to give literal support to the observation that living and working as a teacher in an Indian community demands a twenty-four-hour-a-day interest in the work.

Use of an intermediary provides another way to communicate with the teacher. Parents who could write sometimes sent children to the school with notes for the teacher. The use of notes suggests the social distance that separated the teacher from the rest of the village, for I was not aware of notes being used to any extent in the exchange of information among households. Notes ranged in complexity from lengthy explanations about pupil absence to written requests for medical supplies as terse as: "222's." The following request for Lysol disinfectant was written by a teen-ager for his mother:

> Hi
> There
>   please me "LiE SO"
> Just give him to Alvin.   please and
>   Thank
>   You
>   sign by
>   Mrs. Vera Alfred
> PS   I need it for washe floor.

Teachers, too, have used notes to communicate with villagers. This handwritten note was sent with the first report card of the year by one teacher:

> This is the first report we have issued from the school. Tests will be run shortly, but genarally [sic] each child is now behind in his grade. That each child comes regularly to school, that school operates well, and that each child comes with the idea of learning and behaving is up to Mum & Dad too, not just Teacher. Each boy and girl is with teacher for 5 hrs a day, the rest of his time with parents.

One parent returned the teacher's note with this reply written on the back:

> I signed the report, and have been talking to my son about doing better and

I will help him more. I know how important it is to get education, I only hope and pray the other parents feel the same way. Thank you.

Children frequently came to school with verbal messages. Presumably children were instructed to ask permission to go digging or to take a trip to Alert Bay on a school day. The message was usually delivered more curtly: "I'm going digging," or "My dad said I'm going to the Bay."

Finally, there are formal channels for communication between school and village. Some parents came during school hours or after school to discuss a problem or make a request. I was invited to discuss school at the first band meeting of the new term, and my request for the airing of any problems did provoke a short discussion. When attendance declined in the late spring, I notified the Indian agent and he sent letters to three families advising them that he would withhold their Family Allowance if children did not attend school regularly.

The Indian Affairs Branch provides a report card form for use by teachers. Letter grades are given in subject matter areas and space is provided for teacher comments. When report cards were issued in the village they were signed and returned with dispatch. No question was asked about the meaning of any letter grade or comment.

Although formal parent-teacher conferences are intended by educators to facilitate interaction and mutual understanding, they do not necessarily achieve these ideals when Indian parents and White teachers confer. Judging from both parent and teacher accounts, conferences arranged by village teachers often have done no more than provide teachers with an opportunity to complain about the children, the school, and the village. Because of the taciturn nature of most village adults, visits with them often leave pauses in conversation. Most teachers, by contrast, habitually fill conversational pauses as part of their professional demeanor. The teacher inevitably dominates the conversation. If the parent has a problem and is willing to bring it up at all, it may be cast so modestly that the teacher misses the point. Differences in observations of protocol can become affronts to the teacher or to parents during a conference held either at school or in a village home. After working for years in an Indian village, one local teacher still was unaware that most Indian hosts would never think to ask a visitor to sit down. He complained indignantly, "If my wife went to visit, she had to stand for hours, but if they come in they pick the best chair."

A teacher in a formal parent-teacher conference faces the always difficult problem of what to tell parents about a child as a pupil. To the often heard "How's he doin'?" there are pitfalls regardless of how the teacher responds. If a teacher uses a relative standing among the pupils to evaluate them and discuss their progress, he can free himself of making invidious comparisons with non-Indian pupils, but this can lead to a vast overestimation of the abilities of the better pupils. A young village adult had been told by an enthusiastic teacher that he was smart enough to be a lawyer. His education stopped twelve years short of that goal when the agent summarily suspended him from school for refusing to play in a softball game, but he maintains a rather unrealistic self-image when he insists in any discussion of education, "Oh, I coulda been a lawyer—the teacher said so."

THE BEHAVIOR AND PERCEPTIONS OF TEACHERS

"You can't be friendly here. They've got to know where they stand."

"If we are nice, they don't know their place."

These comments represent one extreme of the range of teacher attitudes. At the other extreme are comments like that made by a young lady at the conclusion of one week in the village teaching for the summer Bible School program: "It seems that all these kids need is someone to love them." Probably most teachers start out with benevolent attitudes. The teacher who made the first remarks explained:

> I wanted to stay here several years, and I decided that I would do it with love. But they were so impertinent. If we were going to stay, we had to be tough. Discipline is based on fear and not on love. They respect me because they are afraid. So I strapped it out. It worked.

Many of the problems which distort teacher perceptions of Indian life and of Indian pupils have no direct bearing on the Indian population itself. The problems reflect isolation, physical inconvenience and hardships, low salaries, lack of training, and the inherent difficulties for any adult working with groups of children within the highly structured framework of the public school. Other insecurities are faced by most teachers in the Indian schools, including an undefined but pervasive defensiveness and a feeling of job insecurity. These insecurities stem in part from the bureaucratic organization in the federal system with its officials, inspections, and regulations. They are compounded by the lack of communication between and among teachers, by the lack of any commonly accepted criteria for judging teacher effectiveness, and by the lack of formal preparation which leads teachers to feel that if they only had more training, their classroom problems would disappear.

Some of the personal insecurities felt by teachers are directly related to the Indian community. Few White teachers coming to a village have experienced being in a minority group before. Some teachers have lived at village schools in a state of perpetual fear, with the material evidence of nailed or boarded windows even if their fears were not expressed overtly. The wife of one teacher had expressed such anxiety about what might happen to her husband if he went about in the village after dark that she refused to let him leave the teacherage in the evening. Such fears are not assuaged by occasional village parties which include incidents of violence.

The teacher's concern for his personal property is a problem which relates directly to Indian-White interaction. During the year five teachers in local day schools suffered losses by theft either of personal property taken from the teacherages or of skiffs and kickers. Two thefts were privately resolved between teachers and villagers, two were reported to the RCMP, and no action was taken on the fifth. A state of psychological depression for the teacher followed most of the thefts, resulting in a lowering of teacher morale and effectiveness and at least a temporary breakdown in school-community relations. At Blackfish Village the school has been broken into so often in past years that the chief councillor expressed surprise when I assured him that no one had broken into the building during my absence at the Christmas holidays. I did not fare as well at Easter.

One teacher at Blackfish forwarded to his anonymous successor a copy of his closing report. His cover letter included these observations:

> My Wife and I are thinking of you poor souls who will be carrying on the Battle at Blackfish Village this year. Whatever They do to the place (and doubtless it will be very little) you can only have a difficult year. My predecessor reacted even more strongly and we learn that his poor wife wept! You will find that little in the way of actual learning has even been achieved. . . . I only hope you know the way around a set of tools, and can survive!
>
> Best of luck?

His report consisted essentially of problems with the school plant, and he cautioned that no teacher can be fairly judged when he must face so many problems. He included some personal reactions to the pupils and to the village:

> The students were very wild on arrival and were obviously unused to normal classroom routine. The parents are in any case apathetic at the best.
>
> . . .
>
> The Village, on arrival from a boat trip, presents the most desolate picture. Neglected shacks in generally filthy state smell profusely when the warm weather breaks through. The children, always filthy, came to respect us. . . .
>
> The children were always most hostile toward everything around the 19th of the month when all the parents left for Minstrel Island or Alert Bay to drink up the Family Allowance Cheque. This Hostility was again apparent when we returned with groceries. My wife could pack heavy boxes in spite of requests for help, and Oil Drums would remain at the Dock unless I rolled them up myself. The Hill is steep and needless to say my back was badly torn about when we returned to the City.

Much of this teacher's antagonism toward villagers was shared by villagers toward him. He conducted classes only intermittently when he arrived at the village, and his reluctance to open school in the face of the water shortage and other maintenance problems was never fully overcome. He did not succeed in developing a daily school routine. Parents claimed that the hour for starting school depended on when the teacher awoke; sometimes school started in the afternoon, and often it did not start at all. He fought a losing battle with attendance and during the last two weeks of school the children refused to attend. He was warned to fulfill his duties more effectually and ultimately his resignation was demanded (personally) by the regional superintendent. A teacher in a nearby school observed, "Fellows like him, they spoil it, because they take those fellows when they can't get others."

One of the expectations for a competent classroom teacher is that he possess the skills and knowledge necessary to assess what his pupils know and what they need to know. Teachers hold this expectation for themselves as part of their specialized knowledge and ability. Newcomers who accept positions as teachers for the Branch are aware that their own standards, based on their experience as pupils and perhaps as teachers in urban schools, may not or will not be appropriate as a basis for judging their Indian pupils. Virtually all teachers preface any statement about their Indian pupils with an acknowledgement that, of course, one must make allowances.

In actually conducting his classroom, however, the teacher has no basis for judging his pupils other than his own experience. To abdicate judgment renders him incompetent in one of the central aspects of his role as he accepts it. To adjust standards implies that standards must be lowered for Indian pupils. Teachers seem equally loath to accept the idea that Indian pupils should be held to an absolute standard as they are loath to accept the contrary, although the question is inevitably posed and argued in these terms.

To the extent that a teacher might wish to reassess his basis for evaluating pupils and to set realistic classroom goals, he is unlikely to find available resources to guide him, reinforcement of his effort, or a sufficiently long-term commitment to his job to warrant his endeavor. Inspectors' visits are too brief to be of help and their own experiences may not have included teaching in small village schools or even teaching Indian pupils. During a teacher's rare visits with fellow teachers there is never time for more than making acquaintances and sharing mutual complaints. The Branch does not orient new teachers concerning either Indian pupils or Indian communities except as individual opportunities arise.[1]

One local teacher during this study set for herself a goal of "catching up" by covering certain curriculum materials. In May she reported that the class had "caught up," a claim she substantiated with the achievement of her pupils on grade-level tests issued by the provincial teachers' federation. Such a report of achievement was most uncommon among teachers. More often teachers abdicate subject matter or grade-level goals in despair and substitute other goals for academic ones. Not infrequently the substitute goal is time—simply waiting for the end of the school year. Other teachers set out to teach literacy skills but after confronting their Indian pupils and some realities of village life they shift to vague and complex value-goals. One teacher at Blackfish wrote: "I will be just as happy if I can see results in a growth of honesty, kindness, consideration, etc. However I think that it is unlikely that there will be great changes." He left after four months in the village and it does seem unlikely that there were any great changes.

With no established criteria for measuring progress or success, classroom and community frustrations begin to mount and to increase teacher anxiety and a sense of failure. What, in the teacher's perception, is the explanation for his problems? Where do teachers place the blame for their lack of success in the classroom?

Teachers blame the government and specifically the education division within the Indian Affairs Branch as one source of their problems. Some teachers complain that immediate supervisors are scarce, inexperienced in Indian education, and relatively ineffective in the bureaucracy. Dissatisfaction is also aimed at the lack of an appropriate curriculum or of guidelines for teachers. As one teacher complained:

> The department should tell the teacher *what to teach*. They should have a curriculum for these schools. The provincial curriculum is easy for them to use, but it doesn't *tell*!! But we need a guide of what to do, not the kind of thing the Inspector is saying, like, "These floors should be polished."

Teachers also see themselves as contributing to their lack of success in the class-

---

[1] Whether orientation and previous classroom experience are essential prerequisites for teaching in village schools is a researchable question which deserves attention. Such a study would provide valuable information for educators in the Indian Affairs Branch.

room through feelings of self-doubt and personal inadequacy in coping with Indian pupils. In one survey of British Columbia's Indian schools the responses from two-thirds of the teachers emphasized the partial or complete failure of some part of their own endeavor (Hawthorn *et al.* 1960:299). To illustrate his despair, a teacher in a neighboring village described what had happened to three sixteen-year-olds who had been his students for several previous years: one had passed conditionally, gone to Alert Bay to continue school, dropped out of school, been raped, and had started to drink heavily; the two others had not passed, and therefore remained in the village with nothing to do, and one of them had also started drinking heavily. The teacher concluded his account with the question, "Am I a failure?"

Another teacher, new to the village, reacted with the typical feeling, "Much of the fault may lie with me" in assessing his problems. He suggested two further factors contributing to teacher problems which most teachers perceive as outweighing both the inadequacies of the Branch and personal inadequacies: problems with parents and problems with pupils. Teacher generalizations about Indian parents, like generalizations about Indian pupils, tend to ignore the range of individual differences and tend to be negative in character. "The parents are more of a problem than the kids," observed one teacher. "They don't really care what goes on in school as long as the lid stays on," observed another.

Village teachers have been aware that the activities carried on in class receive little or no reinforcement in most homes. Few parents ever encourage their children to count objects or to learn color names. Only one village parent reported reading occasionally to her children, and no parent would think of teaching his child to read. Nor did parents direct their children's attention to what it was they hoped was happening in school. Children were usually extolled only to "do good" and to "be good" while in class.

Comforting as it may be to lay the blame upon a host of contributing factors like the parents and the Branch, teachers inevitably face the specific problem of what it is about the Indian child himself that makes him so refractive to classroom learning.

Most teachers at Indian schools will volunteer lengthy explanations of why the learning problems of their pupils do not stem from a lack of inherent ability, although not all local Whites share the view that Indians are as bright as Whites. Still, following the initial difficulty in finding classroom material that is "easy" enough for Indian pupils to do, one of the greatest shocks to new teachers comes when they administer and score a standardized test. In spite of all the things teachers say about the inappropriateness and limits of such tests, about the different backgrounds of their pupils, and about the lack of test sophistication among their pupils, test results seem to stun teachers with empirical, scientific evidence of low pupil ability. Witness the change in this new teacher's attitude in notes received from him in November and then in January, based on his experience in a neighboring village:

> I have some bright students and I mean it. I have some who are average and I have some that are just plain stupid—let's face it, you'll find this in *any* school.

But two months later:

> I have just finished giving all the grades II–VIII I.Q. tests—WOW!—now I know why I usually had the feeling of beating my head against the proverbial brick wall! I have out of 8 students tested, only one I.Q. over 76!! They're all of the near idiot caliber—God! I was bowled over. Then I figured out their respective M.A.'s[2] and this was just another shock wave!!—even my 13–15 year olds have M.A.'s of 10!! How can you stop from lowering your own bloody standards after reading results like this?

Classroom misbehavior is another facet in teacher perceptions of the problems of pupils. This problem may be more severe at Blackfish than in other village schools. One White missionary stated candidly that in his opinion the older children at Blackfish were "more lawless" than in any of the other villages. Another former teacher stated, "This was the worst group I ever taught in my life, White or Indian."

One teacher at Blackfish Village identified three factors, all centering around behavior, which he felt contributed directly to his problems in class:

1. The children seem to have no respect for their elders.
2. They do not seem to be used to doing as they are told.
3. They have little motivation toward learning or behaving at home and little idea of how they will need education in the future.

Children are not "used to doing as they are told" because only the teacher attempts to direct so much behavior by this method. Most of the "telling" a child hears outside the classroom is limited to the phrase "Don't fool around." A parent, older sibling, other villager, or the teacher may receive a response such as "I don't have to," "Why should we?" "You can't tell us what to do, you're not one of the councillors," or "Fuck you, then," to almost any kind of request from "You're supposed to go home," or "You boys are going to get in trouble sucking gas like that," to "Sit down," or "Now put away your books and pencils." Reluctance to do the teacher's bidding bordered on outright refusal at times over such requests as taking out material from one's desk, coming to a table for small-group instruction, or coming into the classroom at the end of recess.

Allied with reluctance to follow teacher direction is the problem of motivation for classroom tasks. In the lore of schoolteaching any pupil who does not move in the direction a teacher aims him is said to lack motivation. The idea is widely shared by teachers of Indian pupils that motivation is a key problem. Instead of following teacher directions and assignments, the children "fool around." One teacher wrote:

> These kids like to joke a lot and fool around a lot and this is one reason for lack of "attention span"—they have the idea they would rather fool around than study—it's not their fault so much as it is their parents. They see them and they see what's in this village life . . . and they get caught up in doing bugger all—they get convinced that it's the thing to do. It's a lark to go to Oakalla [prison] for a 3–6 month stretch—it doesn't carry the stigma we attach to it because they don't live in our society.

---

[2] MA = mental age, a score on an intelligence test expressed as the chronological age at which an average child performs as well as the subject does.

Such fooling around does not necessarily take the form of classroom mischief. It is more of an unhurried view of the cosmos: pupils simply pause to daydream, to draw, or to do almost anything except what the teacher has planned. Coupled with this is the practice of fibbing or telling stories—the "klikwala." The combination of fooling around, taking one's time, and the verbal fooling around of the klikwala work to produce the very opposite of the serious and industrious classroom atmosphere desired by the teacher.

Listening is a classroom problem. "If they are told to do something, they only listen when they feel like it," wrote one teacher. Inattention was so habitual for one pupil that teacher and villagers alike accepted his behavior as the result of a hearing loss until a doctor proved otherwise. As a classroom syndrome the pattern of nonlistening behavior among the pupils might be explained as a mechanism by which children reduce the dissonance of so much teacher-talk in English. However, the same lack of attention is also evident when children are addressed by their parents, particularly if the comments are directives.

"They have never listened to the teacher here. I always tell my boys to listen," one mother reported. Yet her children heard only Kwakwala at home and they were among the least responsive of the pupils to the teacher's questions and directions. Within the class I observed that children not only did not listen to me but failed often to listen to each other either in instruction or in games. When I introduced the game of bingo, a game children age ten and older enjoy and could organize themselves, I was amazed at the lack of attention of some children to the numbers being called. On Valentine's Day many children did not respond when their names were called to receive valentines in spite of the excitement of accumulating them. Occasionally during a teacher discourse pupils clasped their hands over their ears, a behavior which I also observed in a classroom in a neighboring village.

Problems of punctuality and attendance plague teachers in some villages. Attendance forms the basis for a monthly report which teachers submit to the Branch. The report includes a figure representing the percent attendance. Teachers are sensitive to the monthly attendance figure and express suspicion that it is used as a measure of their effectiveness. Offhand remarks by Branch officials suggest a basis for their suspicions. I was told unofficially, "The figure shouldn't be below 85 percent and we have some schools which report almost 100 percent."

At Blackfish Village monthly reports showed a range from 77 percent to 89 percent attendance. These figures mask part of the problem of actual pupil presence in the classroom and of the effect of haphazard attendance on teacher morale and effectiveness. Occasionally school began with only two or three children while other pupils ambled in as late as 11:30 A.M. Yet the persistent tardiness of children from some families did not seem calculated to disrupt the class or to frustrate the teacher. Often pupils who arrived late had exhibited a great deal of self-direction in coaxing themselves to get up, possibly to wash, and to come to school in the absence of any direction or encouragement, sometimes in the absence of any adult in the home. If everyone had made it to class by the midmorning recess, the straggling return after recess took more class time since many children went home for a snack. Home chores interfered with the return after noon, and a recess in the after-

noon often concluded with another slow, reluctant return to class. Parents of habitually tardy or absent pupils always had a variety of excuses. Villagers criticized
these parents and pointed out that when children attend St. Michael's attendance
and punctuality are not problems.

Bullying and tormenting, although rooted in interpersonal and interfamily
conflict within the village, were the source of a great deal of disruptive behavior in
class. Not only was it impossible to prevent bullying in class but often the classroom was the only place where a pupil facing retaliation was away from the protection of his parents or older siblings. There were days when some children sat in
class fearfully anticipating the bullying they would receive as soon as school was
dismissed.

Teacher interference did not reduce bullying and tormenting but sometimes aggravated the situation. Children who were being victimized often begged me not to
interfere. Some parents complained about the problem, but most kept their feelings
to themselves. One parent expressed her concern for her eight-year-old son in a
note written to me from the hospital, although she had never brought up the problem while talking to me at the village:

> I guess my husband worries about him when I'm not there because maybe
> you know about the Duncan kids bullying the other kids and even his own
> cousin likes to bully him sometimes. A lot of times I find out when they do that
> to him and I tell him that I'd report it to you so you can do something about it.
> But he begs me not to tell you, probably because he knows it would be worse
> for him if I did, so I'd just do as he says.

When fights among members of different households resulted in unresolved ill
feelings between families, the pupils most likely to bear further recriminations in
class often absented themselves for several days from school and sometimes from
the village. In the course of the year nineteen pupils missed school out of fear
of bullying. For two pupils threats were given as the reason for leaving the village
school. Joseph claimed that an age-mate had threatened to beat him up if he returned to school again, although he offered no reason for the threat. In November
an eleven-year-old girl came to live in her sister's house at Blackfish Village, partly
to assist with a new baby, partly because of problems with her own parents. She
was tormented constantly in class and in the village, and after Christmas the teacher received the following note from the sister:

> Writing to tell you about Mary. Maybe I shouldn't have let her go home for
> Christmas. But she didn't want to come back. I don't really blame her, the kids
> around here like to bully her. I think Leslie Willie has the same problem.
> Norma and her friends are always trying to beat him up. I heard he sat in Ar-
> nold's house all morning. I don't know why Mrs. Willie doesn't do anything
> about it.

Older children occasionally direct younger ones, especially siblings, to carry out
their commands in class, perhaps to take some coveted material but more often to
perform some minor act of aggression against another young child. Such bullying
by proxy set up an impenetrable circularity for the teacher in the cause and effect of
classroom misbehavior. To illustrate: Reggie came crying to me in class com-

plaining that Archie Duncan, just a fraction bigger and tougher, had hit him. Archie's big brother, Gary, had told him to, explained Archie, "because Reggie had been cheeky to Gary." One teacher felt she had identified how an Indian mother reacts to such a situation—the mother always advises a younger child to keep out of the way or not to provoke an older, bigger one. The teacher reported some success with her class in using this approach which placed responsibility on the younger children not to antagonize the older ones.

In an attempt to identify the social structure within the classroom, and to see if a different seating arrangement within the class might alleviate some of the bullying, I administered two sociometric-choice tests. Pupils were asked to choose children with whom they preferred to sit, and to note if there were pupils with whom they preferred not to sit. The choices were tabulated and were plotted on a sociometric matrix. An examination of the matrix suggested that the children held clear and stable patterns of friendship choices. There were many mutual choices and many mutual rejections. Rejection appeared to be a method by which class members were held in line. For example, the three most frequently chosen members of the class, the two oldest boys and a popular twelve-old-year boy, rejected the two older girls, although the girls were clearly in the top interacting group of the class. The younger pupils tended not to be as aware of the structure of friendships and made less discriminating choices.

Reseating as suggested by sociometric choices did little to minimize conflict within the classroom. The irony of having school officials encourage the attendance of Indian pupils and then deny or make light of the importance of the quarreling and taunting, the "physical and verbal torture" that drives children out of school, is a serious concern in Indian education (Wax *et al.* 1964:45). The problem remained unresolved during my year at the village.

Teacher perceptions of their Indian pupils and of classroom problems are not limited to those described above but each problem identified here is a serious one in any classroom and each has been a significant problem at the Blackfish Indian Day School.

6 / The pupils and the classroom

DOROTHY WROTE THIS account in September to try to help me to understand my pupils:

Some children from here do not like school. It's hard for me to explain why because I like school. I'll try to write some at the same time any way. The children when they are late say they didn't hear the bell. But today I proved to myself they could hear the bell. I was at Joseph Willie's home this after noon on an errand. When the bell rang I could hear it even if I were in our home. The second reason I think is they are just dumb and don't know what we do in class.

My initial impression was that village pupils attended school reluctantly and ritually. Children expect to be at school but their participation is analogous to traveling on someone else's boat: one gets on, sits patiently during the long, slow ride, and eventually gets off. Age sixteen is the destination of the educational journey. No precedent existed at the village for any other conclusion to one's formal education, for Blackfish school has never "graduated" a student.

Previous teachers seem to have felt secure in promoting a pupil as long as he was to remain in the village school, but there is no record of a student completing the work of the day school and officially going on to grade eight or nine at Alert Bay. Few young people in the village who reached the seventh grade remained for the entire school year; those who did inevitably repeated grade seven, grade eight, or both. It was suggested earlier that teachers in village schools grope for ways to evaluate the progress of their Indian pupils. Within the multi-graded village classroom, promotions in the lower grades pose no administrative problem, for the assigned grade does not have to match the assigned tasks. Continued annual promotions eventually force the question of whether to promote a pupil beyond the village school. Records of promotions indicate that teachers have been uniformly unwilling to make such an endorsement of their pupils.

Getting out of school eventually becomes a matter of time for a pupil even if earlier promotions came annually. Although pupils have occasionally quit school on the day of their sixteenth birthday, they have more often dropped out of school the year before they reached the age of sixteen. Most children anticipate that their schooling will terminate upon attaining a certain age rather than upon completion

95

of a specific grade. This attitude is illustrated in a comment made to me by a twelve-year-old pupil, although she was incorrect about the age at which she will be able to quit. She staggered along the road one evening pretending to be drunk and said as she passed, "Mr. Wolcott, I won't be at school tomorrow. I'm twenty-one now, so I don't have to go any more."

As a waiting game, school was often described by children as a boring place. Norma and Dorothy noted this in their daily writing. Norma's entries during the latter part of the school year often included a reference to her boredom in school and her wish to quit, such as this comment in May:

> Today is Friday. It is the last day of school for the week. I'm anxious for 3:00 o'clock. I'm sick and tired of school.

Boredom was also discussed by the youths who had left school. To escape from boredom seemed to be the reason that prompted Joseph and his age-mate to return to school late in October. When I asked why they wished to return, Joseph's friend laughed self-consciously and said, "To get an education, I guess." When the idleness of October was followed by an opportunity in November to start digging clams, the boys left school once again.

The decision whether he will be promoted or retained at the same grade at the end of the term may seem mystic or capricious to the young pupil. Older children and adults associate promotions with completing texts identified for certain grade levels. The pupils were sensitive about the level of material with which they worked. My initial overestimation of their ability made it necessary for me to recall certain texts and to distribute ones at lower grade levels. Even though the children were unable to do the work in the higher grade books they resented my reassigning them to lower grade ones.

The discussion of pupil attitudes which follows is based primarily on the written responses of older pupils to topics of a projective nature. At most fourteen children could give written responses to the kinds of questions dealt with here; usually the number of responses is even fewer. Among this group, referred to here as the older pupils, every child projected either living in the village as an adult or at least maintaining close ties with it. For example, Norma included the possibility of living in Campbell River or even in Vancouver when she gets married but she hoped her family would always be at Blackfish Village.

Eight of the group of older pupils wrote on the theme "What I Would Like To Be Doing Ten Years From Now." Such a projection in time is not a customary kind of thinking among the children, and one boy could not imagine doing more than going to Kingcome Inlet to swim. Norma imagined that she would probably be married by the time she had reached her twenties and she entertained the possibility of getting married "next year." She also mentioned the possibility of continuing in school, in which case she thought she would like to be a secretary or a nurse. "I haven't maked up my mind yet," she wrote. Dorothy chose the same alternatives and also included teaching as a possible vocation. If she were to become a teacher she thought she would "stick around Blackfish Village for a couple of years." A year younger than Norma, Dorothy seldom expressed the same concern with boys or with marriage that Norma did, and she started her response with, "I don't know if I'll get married or not. I think I'll be an old maid."

A twelve-year-old girl's answer to what she would like to be doing ten years hence was contained in one sentence, "I would like to be at Blackfish Village." The five boys who responded also implied or stated that they would still be at the village. Walter wrote, "I would be in jail from now on." All of his brothers beyond school age spent some time in jail during the year, so there is some basis for his projection. At another time he had written, "When I grow up I think I should like to be a clam digger and fishing." In conversation most boys projected a life as a fisherman for themselves. A fifteen-year-old mentioned joining the army as a future possibility although he had no information as to how he would go about enlisting or whether there were any prerequisites; no villager has been in the army.

The older pupils were asked to write their recollections of previous teachers. I had hoped to identify prevailing attitudes toward all teachers in their accounts. Instead, recollections tended to be of specific incidents, usually of especially pleasant occasions or of occasions of particular strife between the pupils and the teacher. The recollections about one teacher were all unfavorable as these excerpts from three pupils suggest. Norma wrote:

> The first day of school he rang the bell about ten o'clock. He said his watch stopped. And he kept ringing it ten o'clock. We hardly worked. We just draw when we get in class. When I used to ask him to help me. He used to give me a wrong answer. He isn't a schoolteacher. He's a piano teacher. He used to make excuses on school days. He used to say he's got a cold or a bad headache.

A twelve-year-old boy recalled:

> All what we do is read and spelling and draw. Do you know what I call him I call him stupid teacher. We didn't even had a Christmas party and a Santa Claus and we didn't get our report cards.

To describe what he remembered about this teacher, one fourteen-year-old boy gave the following account of a fight between the teacher and the pupils:

> The teacher told me to Do the spelling and arithmetics and work book. We our late and he try strapped us with Jack and Walter and Gary always cry. Just I try hit Gary nose, and the teacher try mad us Gary has got a bleeding nose. I never get cry. The teacher try to beat Joseph and Larry hit his eye and I kick his feet and arm and his ass and his wife try to stop us I kick so hard.

Another recent teacher was remembered more favorably. The children recalled treasure hunts with cash prizes which he had often conducted. He is also remembered for dances held, according to the children, as often as three times a week. One girl wrote:

> We dance at night time. We do reading and arithmetic spelling test. He was our best teacher. We treasure hunt every Friday.

A boy who had been in grade two at the time wrote:

All I like to do is read and I like to play blocks and he like to gave us pop-sicles and I like to paint and draw.

Few children could remember more than two or three previous teachers. Walter's recollections of one of his earlier teachers were positive:

He and she used to smoke eulachons. What I like to do when he and she was here spelling and arithmetics book "C" and book "B" and handwriting and he used to tell story for us at recess outside. We used to have fun [in Walter's spelling, "we yus to half fun"]. He used to let us in the basement when it's raining in day time. He used to like red cod. We used to have a Halloween Party, Christmas Party. He used to play with his violin. He used to try to learn me how but I can't learn it. I also like Ronnie and Norman [his sons] because we used to go and chop trees down and make a raft. We used to have fun that time. He was a good teacher. I love him.

Good-by.

In spite of the positive recollections of two of their three previous teachers, the children's attitude toward the teacher role tends to be a negative one. This seemed to be an attitude learned within the classroom, and I felt there was a more hostile attitude toward school among older pupils than among younger ones. Parents of children who were beginners in school noted behavior changes in their offspring. One six-year-old described to his family how the older children directed him to misbehave in class. Reggie's father expressed concern shortly after bringing Reggie to the village that Reggie was getting "cheeky" like the older children and that he no longer listened at home.

The attitudes and actions of pupils from different families toward the teacher's authority were similar to the attitudes toward authority generally shared in their families. Several of the older pupils were from families which the RCMP said were continually in trouble; these children tended to resent any authority, including that of the teacher. The few families who looked upon the RCMP, the Indian agent, and health officials as dependable allies were the ones whose children were among the youngest pupils. Perhaps the attitudes of these younger pupils toward the classroom and teacher would have been more positive under other conditions, but as the youngest and smallest pupils they were quickly socialized by their classmates into the pattern of reluctant submission characteristic of the older pupils. The attitude toward the teacher's authority extended to all official school visitors. As the children watched the district superintendent walk about the classroom and look at different children's work, Norma stated to me, "He's not going to look in *my* books!"

Five older pupils wrote on the topic, "If I Were the Teacher." All five envisioned a daily program almost identical to the one then being used in the classroom. A boy who identified closely with the teacher at the beginning of the school year even included what he would do at noontime: "During lunch I'd think what's good to do in class. When I eating I read the paper they did that morning. Then I'll go in to the class then write what I planned." The pupils described how they would deal with children who came to school late or dirty, who did not finish their work, or who did not pass tests. The following excerpts from Norma's writing include all the possible discipline problems she anticipated and the punishments she would assign. Although she shared my perception of some classroom problems and annoyances, not one of the disciplinary methods she suggests was used during the year:

> . . . if anybody's late, they have to write hundred lines. And keep the toilet clean. Their clothes clean and comb hair. . . . And if nobody works they get a strapping. . . . And if they get the room dirty they'll sweep the whole classroom. . . . And if anybody talks back. They'd get a strapping. If they get out of their desk they'll have to write lines. If they don't ask permission to sharpen their pencil they'll get strapping. If they wear hats and kerchiefs in class they'll have to stand in corner for one hour with their hands on their heads. . . . If they make a noise in class, they all stay in for half an hour. If anybody talks in class they write lines about hundred lines. If anybody's absent they have lots of homework for the next day. And if anybody fights they get a strapping.

Dorothy's expectations for behavior were also strict: "I'd like my class to be very quiet. If not they would get a strapping from me." By contrast, her attitude toward academic performance is permissive:

> I would give them tests before Christmas, Easter, and the final tests at June. After the tests, if anyone fails, I would ask them to tell me why. For example if one of my pupils did fail I'd tell that child to write on a paper to tell me why. If that child has a good excuse, I'd tell that child to "smarten up" and pay attention to his or her work more.
>
> I would go to see their parents to see if they have a normal living, like if they go to sleep before nine o'clock, have good meals every day.
>
> Yes sir! If I were the teacher. A lot of changes would be made around here at Blackfish Village. The children would have to listen even if I were a girl teacher.

Part of the children's perception of school as a "boring" place may be due to their experience with long, tedious assignments designed by harassed teachers to keep them occupied for extended periods of class time. The older children expected and sought this kind of busy work. In the absence of such assignments they sometimes asked for highly repetitive work like copying words or redoing review pages of number combinations. Their experience has led them to equate classroom learning with endless repetition.

The actual behavior accorded me by the pupils is another source of data on pupil attitudes toward the teacher, albeit a more subjective source than their written comments. At times I was cussed at, threatened, challenged, and spit on. My classroom directives were often ignored, and my classroom actions and comments were variously greeted with laughter, silence, sullenness, or tears. Yet while I was often defied, I was sometimes defended. Occasionally an older child, particularly a sibling, ordered a young pupil to "Listen to the teacher" (sometimes accompanying the directive with a cuff on the head) or gave a direction in Kwakwala on my behalf. At best I was liked, listened to, confided in, my approval was sought for effort in classwork, and I was the recipient of things the children wished to share. Having taught young urban children, I was not surprised at the ways the youngest pupils acted out anger or negative feelings toward me, but I had not expected the older pupils to act out their feelings in similar fashion. The older villager pupils seemed less suppressed in their expression of both positive and negative feelings in class then my urban pupils had been.

The children worked to socialize me just as I was attempting to socialize them. Their expectations were sometimes made explicit. Delayed by the local air service one Monday morning after a weekend away, I did not get to the village until after nine o'clock, the usual hour for beginning school. The children showed no enthusiasm at my arrival and there was no tolerance for my tardiness. A sixteen-year-old boy yelled across the village as I rang the bell, "Why don't ring that thing in the afternoon, for Chrissake." More than once the children expressed some anger at my drinking with villagers, even if it was with their own parents. "But you're the teacher," they reminded me. Few children would accept the case I tried to make for social drinking, although at least one girl acknowledged:

Mr. Wolcott was in our house when Lena and them were drinking. Mr. Wolcott was drinking too, but he never got drunk.

The children taught me not to talk much in class, not to give so many orders, not to interfere with their social relationships, not to "force" hard work on them, and to make the best of whatever situation existed. They never let me veer far from what they expected in the way of a routine approach to classroom work. I had always to be "the teacher" in class—a person who "knows everything" and who directs a very narrow range of classroom activities. Occasionally a discussion would catch their interest, but variation in routine was more likely to produce comments like, "We didn't come to school for this, we came to do our schoolwork." I introduced materials from the "modern math" and the older pupils raced through them so they could do their regular arithmetic. They worked at various reading tasks and wrote their personal stories every day of school, yet they were concerned because we never "had language" or used the language books. We expanded our classroom library, but the children were satisfied that they were "having reading" only when they struggled with pedantic readers and workbooks that were virtually impossible for them to complete without constant teacher assistance.

The primary method by which the pupils attempted to socialize me was to exhibit reluctance in complying with my requests. Occasionally this meant a complete refusal to act. At other times they mimicked my behavior or repeated my directions verbatim. There were occasional threats to "tell on" me or to send a parent or older sibling to school to even a score, and one older boy invited me to "come outside and settle it." When the children did not wish to speak explicitly of what they expected of a teacher, they communicated the information in the daily writing which they often used as a way of addressing me. Most frequently such comments dealt with my disciplining, but any behavior on my part was subject to scrutiny. For example, one day I brought first-aid materials into class to patch up a knee instead of taking the child into the teacherage as I usually did. A twelve-year-old girl labored a long while to write:

today mr wolcott bring the bandage in the class you [not] supposed to bring it in here you supposed leave it in your house not in hear you think you are a nurse mr wolcott you are a teacher now you not a nurse

After school closed for the summer I felt that my behavior toward the children became more relaxed and casual. I was not aware of any change in the behavior of the children toward me. When I left the village at the end of summer, several children began to correspond with me. By then I was an old friend while new teachers carried on what one Blackfish teacher referred to as "the battle." Letters to me included comments like this from a boy who attended a provincial school the following year:

> I miss you a lot. . . . And wish you would be back. You were my best teacher in all my grades. . . . My teacher here oh! She mean. Not like you a kind-hearted.

Another pupil wrote from the village:

> I miss you a lot our teacher name is mr———— he is no good for me.

THE CLASSROOM IN MOTION

With the intent of minimizing tardiness and bullying, I began school by a walk through the village in which I was joined by the children who were ready. One purpose for this walk was that parents could tell me if a family had overslept or if children would be late for other reasons. This idea helped punctuality, it cut down excuses about not being able to hear the handbell, and there was a certain public relations feature, I hoped, in having the villagers see the teacher on duty each morning. In spite of the plan, the families with the largest number of children in class were still the least punctual.

Daily enrollment ranged from nineteen to twenty-nine pupils of ages six to sixteen and grades one to eight. Thirty-one different pupils enrolled during the year. There were always twice as many boys enrolled. By the end of the year three of the oldest pupils had dropped out of school, each for the last time. One pupil had returned to her home village because of tormenting by the other children. One six-year-old dropped out of school by mutual agreement between teacher and parents because she seemed immature and unhappy as a beginner. Two school-age boys drowned. As a consequence of the drowning accident, in which three village parents were also lost, another schoolchild was sent to live permanently at St. Michael's.

I shared the feeling with other local teachers that a class size of twenty pupils, particularly in a one-room school, is the maximum number with which a teacher can work effectively. Other observers have recommended even smaller classes after noting that in large classes teachers cannot come to know their Indian pupils and communicate with them, but instead spend their time either establishing discipline or trying to elicit scholastic responses (Wax *et al.* 1964:102). In branch schools a second teacher is not authorized until attendance reaches thirty-five. In the villages such an assignment is only theoretical unless a spouse will take the extra assignment, since there is usually no housing for another teacher family regardless of pupil enrollment.

Ninety percent attendance or better for the year was achieved by nine students including Dorothy and Walter. I was discouraged when seven children did not enroll during the first two weeks of school, but June attendance did not diminish as it often had in the past. Year-long attendance today is accepted as part of village life. Contrast this with the recollection of a teacher who taught at Blackfish Village in the mid-thirties:

> Although the year was supposed to follow the school calendar, this school did not open much before the end of October simply because no one had returned to the village until then. The peak enrollment was over the winter months of December, January, and February. As soon as the weather improved in the spring the families would get the wanderlust or start to leave permanently. If I remember correctly the highest number I had the first year was twelve and the second year, fifteen. I would begin and end the school year with three or four.

Once the pupils were inside the classroom their behavior became one of my major problems. I used verbal admonishments and attempted to minimize frustration by not assigning academic tasks that were too difficult. Children who seemed too disruptive or recalcitrant were dismissed from the classroom, usually for that morning or afternoon period. This was intended to minimize my frustration and hostility as well as to eliminate the immediate possibility of further anger or misbehavior. In the children's vocabulary this was termed "being chased out." There was some confusion because being chased out had been used as a final measure by previous teachers while I employed it for the express purpose of preventing such an ultimatum.

For the youngest children, being chased out was often a blessing on days when nothing seemed to be going well between themselves and either their classmates or their teacher. For older pupils such disciplinary action had more negative overtones, perhaps because of being excluded, perhaps because of repercussions at home, perhaps because ultimately there was one thing that the teacher could tell a pupil to do—he could insist that a pupil leave the classroom. The boys in one family received a parental spanking if it was discovered that they had been chased out, and it usually was discovered because other siblings reported it with glee. For Norma and Dorothy, being chased out was a drastic measure and they seemed as anxious as the teacher to avoid a crisis. Each girl revealed her perceptions in writing following the rare incidents when either was sent out. Norma described how in her home the interpretation of her having been chased out one morning was that now she would have to go to school elsewhere:

> . . . this morning it didn't turn out the way it usually turns out that the teacher wants it. So I hope it turns out this afternoon and tomorrow morning. My oldest brother said to me this morning when I went home when Mr. Wolcott told me to go home. My brother said I'm going to St. Michael's.

One morning during the short time that Joseph attended school several of the older pupils, including Joseph, Norma, and Dorothy, failed to return to class at the end of recess, a problem that was becoming more acute each morning. When they did eventually return, I told them they were too late and I would not admit them for the rest of the morning. Dorothy described the problem from her point of view that afternoon:

> Today is a very horrible day for Norma and me. Of course we would be trea-ten as babies. When we are late in this dump the teacher would tell us to come back in the afternoon. There was Larry, Joseph, Norma, Archie, Jack, Terry, and me. Norma got in trouble too, of course. My brother would tell on me that brat. Norma and me made a plan for this week, but it's a secret. This is a strict world for some of us. I thought this was a free world. Norma and me can't even go on Larry's boat; and for me I'm not aloud to go to their house! My brother said I was in my aunties house. I guess thats why I ain't aloud in their. All the time I was in Sarah's house. The teacher is so lazy to ring the bell I guess he expects us to hear him when he calls us. That's all!!

Occasionally children were told to put their heads down on their desks as a class-room disciplinary measure. One girl wrote out her feeling that not being admitted to class was too severe a punishment for tardiness:

> today mr wolcott didn't let us in this dinner what will you do if I was teach mr wolcott I wouldnt chase you away I will tell you to put your head down

A final observation on discipline, written in December by Norma:

> Carol was chased out today. So was Dorothy's brother and Toby Duncan. The teacher's pretty strict today. He won't let anybody get out of there desk, not inless he says so. He's getting stricter every day.

Daily classwork usually began with a long period for various kinds of reading and related seatwork. About midmorning we had indoor calisthenics, followed by an outdoor recess if weather permitted or a free playtime in the large basement. After recess the primary children who had completed their assigned tasks had a choice of playing with blocks, clay, or puzzles, or of drawing or easel painting. Upper-grade pupils wrote their daily notes and then studied formal spelling. The morning ended with a storytime for the younger pupils while older ones finished work, listened to the story, or worked individually at their desks reading or draw-ing.

The afternoon began with an arithmetic lesson followed by an activity like hand-writing at the close of the period. At two o'clock the youngest children were dis-missed. By regulation they are supposed to remain in school far longer, but such a regulation seemed insensitive to their age, their interest in school, and to the prob-lems facing a teacher in a one-room school.[1] With the younger children out of the class there was a final work period used variously for social studies, science, indoor games, art, and individualized reading. The sequence and content of the daily pro-gram came to be accepted to the point where changes had to be arbitrated before they were allowed without pupil resentment.

Only a few children at any given moment were actually working at assigned

---

[1] In their study of contemporary Sioux education, the Waxes recommend: ". . . the pres-ent (nine to four) day of classwork might well be shortened for the benefit of the children, especially the young. The present assumption that confinement within the school building is equivalent to education simply means a lot of wasted time in the classroom: Neither children nor teachers are capable of that sustained study" (*Wax et al.* 1964:109).

tasks. Others sat and watched the teacher or utilized the methods that classroom pupils have to communicate with each other. Short written assignments from the board produced more dependable results than indefinite assignments like "go on with your workbooks" or "reread the story." There seemed too little opportunity for either brief periods of uninterrupted small group instruction or for timely reinforcement of small quantities of correct work to encourage pupils to proceed further.

The only recorded observation of the class by an outsider was the "school inspector's report" made by the district superintendent after a morning visit in the classroom in March. His official report included the following:

> Seating is of conventional plan. . . . The day's assignments and time table are combined on one page. Register is maintained up-to-date. . . . [The teacher is] satisfactorily groomed. Quiet manner, to which pupils have responded. On an earlier visit one could sense the hostility of pupils to school and teachers in general.
>
> .   .   .
>
> Lessons were observed in reading—pupils speak out but read rather haltingly. In the short P.E. period it was gratifying to notice the eagerness and willingness with which pupils participated. Much of the instruction is of an individual nature.
>
> .   .   .
>
> Pupils are still shy and do answer quietly, but are willing to try. Some of the ideas expressed in written work are surprising. In spite of the progress made—chiefly in attitude and desire to try and cooperate—the actual achievement has still a long way to go. . . .

In meeting their classroom assignments the pupils interpreted their tasks as a matter of group as well as of individual concern. This had one major advantage in that for many tasks pupils paired off and completed assignments in informal competitions. Norma and Dorothy worked this way on virtually every subject, comparing numbers of pages completed in a given period, numbers of spelling words correct, or speed in filling up a composition book with personal stories. Dorothy's brother and another boy motivated each other in periods of work and periods of nonwork in their sixth grade effort. A group of fifth-grade boys motivated Walter to keep slightly ahead of them in class assignments. No pupil, however, worked in such a way that another peer was *too* much slower.

The motivating effect of their self-imposed competition was more than offset from the teacher's point of view by the tendency of pupils constantly to help each other, especially for older pupils to help younger ones to the extent of doing all the work designed for the young pupils and ignoring their own. A young pupil literally had no need and no opportunity to discover a new number combination or to identify some known element in a new word. The instant after the teacher posed any such question to a group of younger pupils the answer would be whispered somewhere else in the classroom by the older ones.

The extent of mutual help greatly complicated an accurate teacher assessment of each child's ability and level of achievement. Children worked each other's workbooks and papers, they made complete entries in each other's writing books, and they wrote letters for each other when the class corresponded with pen pals. In administering a standardized test to three brothers I chastised one boy for helping his little brother with the test, whereupon he stopped giving help in English but started helping in Kwakwala. On one occasion eight children, responding to a sentence-completion writing assignment, produced four sets of paired answers. Most writing assignments gave evidence of a similar pairing of responses. The oldest boy in class was so used to having difficult reading words whispered to him by his reading mates that often he did not look in his book at all. He started "reading" in a fourth grade book at the beginning of the year; it was a long while before I realized that he could read independently only at the grade one level. In May I recorded in my notes: "He gets so much help from other kids in subjects that I still doubt that I know his own capabilities."

To the extent that the motivation for seeking and giving so much help stemmed from the inability to answer teacher questions, work the problems, or remember a certain number of spelling words, it was possible to pare down the assignment or level of difficulty. However, the helping extended not only to classroom behavior but also to kibitzing in Kwakwala during games played at the teacherage in the evening and to kibitzing, helping, or sometimes taking over for another person in many village situations. The children's attention focused on the task to be done, whether it was winning at cards or completing an arithmetic paper, and with their combined resources they accomplished the task. As the teacher I felt I had accomplished little when I found that papers assigned to beginners had been completed by pupils twice their age.

There were other complications in assessing levels of achievement. The most recent record of promotion at the school was a list left by a teacher two years earlier. The register for the previous year was missing for the first eight months of school; it finally turned up in a neighboring village. At the large residential schools some pupils literally get "lost in the grades" and return to the same grade for several years. With the annual teacher turnover and lack of communication between one teacher and the next, the same thing has occurred at Blackfish Indian Day School. There were at least four recent instances where a pupil had spent part or all of three succeeding years in the same grade. Every returning pupil in September 1962, had been held back at least one year. In the federal report only two of fourteen boys and two of six girls were in the "normal" age range for their grades.

My pupils and I shared a lack of knowledge about what grade they were in. Two unwritten rules interferred with the determination of grade-level assignment: first, no student was obligated to report his own most recently passed grade, "You're supposed to know, you're the teacher"; second, no student would say what grade another child belonged in, "Ask him." Two of the older fifth-grade boys protested loudly when I suggested that, based on their age, their size, and their ability, they could be in grade six.

At the opening of school Dorothy was "not sure" whether she had been promoted to grade seven the previous year at St. Michael's. A written inquiry to Alert Bay brought this note from the new principal of the day school there:

> There was no promotion list of passes and failures left in this school for the grade 6s so it is impossible to say whether Dorothy passed or failed.

Dorothy wanted to work at the higher grade and she was successful in doing grade seven work during the year. It was not until a month before the close of school that she remembered whether she had passed the previous year. She had not.

Only two upper-grade girls expressed any interest in report-card grades, one of these motivated by a promise of her older sister of a dollar reward for any "A's." Even promotion seemed of slight interest since, except for Dorothy and Norma who were to attend grade eight in Alert Bay, other promotions were only within the classroom. At the end of the semester sixteen of the twenty-two pupils were promoted. In the absence of any official policy, my own policy was that children should keep moving through the grades when possible unless a promotion would separate them from a group of lower-grade students with whom they were well matched. I rationalized that the farther each of these children can go in school the greater his commitment may be to encourage his own children as pupils.

Toward the end of the school year I asked eight of the older children to write what they had liked and had not liked about school during the year. Spelling was the most frequently named favorite subject. Reading and the weekly library hour were mentioned by four pupils. The teacher was named first as what they liked about school by three children, two of whom collaborated in their answer, "This is what I remember Mr. Wolcott. Your nice to us." There were three nominations each for arithmetic, for playing various field games, and for drawing. Swimming, daily writing, and the calisthenics period were each included by two students. Swimming had no relation to classwork but by late spring it was an inevitable entry in any discussion of things children enjoyed doing. Two negative responses were included. Norma began: "I liked school this year. But I'm really tired of school for the last two months." Walter had one complaint: "I don't like the division. That's the only thing I don't like but I like to learn it and would next year I hope."

The pupils considered art activities as one of the more pleasant classroom tasks and they were willing and even insistent about remaining after school to complete art work. Under Norma's and Dorothy's influence younger girls often drew and colored geometric patterns. Boys drew Indian designs, especially killer whales, airplanes, speedboats, and seiners. The youngest boys slavishly drew hull after hull in their sketch books, learning to imitate the accepted standard of the older boys in drawing a seine boat. Margins of written assignments were often decorated. Drawings by the children exhibit attention to detail and a tendency to fill spaces with additional designs or, especially in drawings of animals, to draw additional faces in tails, fins, and wings, a characteristic of traditional native art. One crayon drawing of a whale made by a fourteen-year-old boy contained eighteen design faces within the outline of the whale.

Games and toys introduced for the younger children proved popular with all students. Blocks and primary puzzles for the six- and seven-year-olds were constantly commandeered by older pupils. In the manner of mutual help described above, older pupils often "took over" puzzles in order to work them. It became necessary to provide at least one period a week when older pupils could play uninterrupted by younger ones. In block play the children most often made boats. The older boys usually concluded their play by building battleships which in turn destroyed their other creations and those of their cohorts.

In class we acted out plays and stories on some occasions when classroom morale was high and there was a likelihood that children would willingly take part. In such play the older children tended to inhibit the spontaneity of the younger ones, but there were flashes of creativity in the way pupils identified with their parts. Such behavior by the children first became apparent to me at the village Halloween party in which many children engagingly assumed the role appropriate to their costume. Roles in pantomime were especially popular and well acted.

The most highly motivated classroom project of long duration was an exchange of letters between older pupils and a sixth-grade class in California. Competition developed to see who could receive and send the most letters, and pupils begged to write letters "instead of doing school work."

Many of the entries children made in their daily writing were in the nature of letters to me. Their motivation to write for my immediate consumption spurred long entries, while imaginative stories and fantasy were never attempted. No limits were imposed on what pupils could write, and they could always choose to tell me (in writing) they did not wish to write that day.

Walter was inclined to make every entry a personal note to me. The content of the notes depended upon the state of our relationship at the moment, particularly if he had recently been chastised:

> Mr. Wolcott always make me mat this morning wene I was doing my arithmetics I was mat to this morning me and Leslie and Tommy. G I was mat this Mr Wolott you met me mat. . . .

This entry was written early in the school year:

> I don't like Mr. Wolcott
> he always make me
> work I hate Mr. Wolcott
> I like Mr. Wolcott
> I love Mr. Wolcott
> I like to go to school
> I Like Mr. Wolcott to learn me how

During the year Walter's messages became longer and even more direct, and he wrote out his feelings about many classroom incidents. This entry was his reaction to my having taken away an apple which he had planned to eat in class:

> Dear Mr. Wolcott,
> We were packing wood yesterday me and Raymond were packing lots of wood. Oh, you little monkey, little asshole you got my apple why don't you mind your own business you think you smart little asshole. Goodbye, that's all I can say now. Goodbye, no more writing because you throw my apple.

Several children developed formulas for writing, usually by listing daily the names of their friends preceded with an introduction such as "I like to play tag with . . ." Any variation from this pattern was almost always a direct communication with the teacher, such as this entry of a fourteen-year-old boy following a recess period:

> Mr. Wolcott I kick the ball up the roof Mr Wolcott what can do for him wait for the wind blow   Your story Mr Wolcott

Listening to stories read aloud appealed to most children, provided there was some option about listening and that the stories were not difficult to follow. Stories which could be completed in a few minutes were the most popular, and stories intended for the little children received the best attention from the older pupils as well.

Possibly older children looked forward to school as a place of relative quiet. The classroom play activities of the youngest children were often distracting to older pupils. One boy wrote out his annoyance in a rare example of containment, for usually the action suggested here would have been discharged on impulse:

> Archie and Jimmy are playing blocks they are making lot of noise in school. I can't stand the noise. I feel like slugging them.

In their written comments the older pupils recommended that I put the younger ones in the adjoining classroom. Norma wrote: "If I had a fourteen-year-old in my class she or he would take care of grade one and two. And I'd take care of three to eight." Apparently past teachers have employed this practice. I was able to get some help from older pupils in this manner, but there were limits to its effectiveness. The older children exhibited a reluctance to help, and there were comments from parents that the little children were being bullied or were afraid of the older pupils.

School provided almost the only opportunity to play games of soccer and Indian baseball with a large number of players, and such games were frequently organized by the children at recesses. A rather unexpected interest developed in a classroom program of physical fitness, particularly among the boys of ages ten to fourteen. The number of push-ups and sit-ups which each child could do was recorded and most children tried to surpass their own records. A similar spirit of competition prevailed in the monthly measure of height. Growth of three-quarters of an inch to three and three-quarters inches during the nine months was recorded, and height graphs kept by each child were scrutinized by peers.

Individual recognition and attention from the teacher usually produced positive results but did not always do so. I avoided using comparisons and teacher-induced competition as a source of motivation among the pupils since my efforts did not have the same effect as the competitions which the pupils fostered among themselves. That instances of pupil embarrassment resulting from teacher remarks did occur, as they do in all classrooms, is evident in a fourteen-year-old's description following one period of calisthenics:

> Today we had exercise all the other children were doing it to it was hard. I was the first one. I didn't no what to do. All the children were laughing at me and I got red.

MEASURES OF CLASSROOM PERFORMANCE

The usual precautions which precede a discussion of test data are particularly germane here. The standardized tests used in schools are designed for and normed among urban middle-class pupils. Those test items which discriminate among village pupils (i.e., items which some but not all children answer correctly) may distinguish differences in mental ability, but they may only distinguish the extent of the opportunity each child has had for experiences and contact with the mainstream of urban society. For example, the responses of the children to one item show the extent of their variation, and the variation in turn suggests the possible ambiguity of the item. On this test children select from among three pictured objects the object that best "goes with" two given ones. The two given objects in this instance are pictures of a turkey on a platter and of a loaf of sliced bread. Pupils answer by selecting among pictures of a dish, a knife, or several pieces of fruit. Among twenty-two village pupils three selected the dish, five selected the knife, four placed marks on both the dish and the knife, nine selected the fruit, and one pupil did not mark an answer.

I was told that the average (mean) IQ of pupils in provincial schools in British Columbia is 110. No child tested in the village attained a score as high as 110 on any test or on any part of a test. A descriptive classification accompanying one of the two standardized tests given to the entire class showed by comparison with the groups on which the test was normed that of the twenty-two village children tested, three pupils were of average intelligence, six were dull normal, seven were borderline, and six were mental defectives. Regardless of teacher sophistication, the negative tone of such labels affects both teacher assessment of pupils and teacher morale.

In support of the tests, they did rank children consistently and the ranking was generally consistent with the teacher's assessment of classroom performance. The results of one test were also consistent with the pupils' own estimates of the ability of their peers. Pupils identified eight of the highest performers when asked to write the names of the ten pupils they believed had "done the best" for their age, including (correctly) the name of the youngest pupil.

The Indian Affairs Branch cooperates with the provincial department of education in a testing program in all British Columbia schools at the seventh-grade level. The test distributed for seventh-graders was the Lorge-Thorndike, Level Four. This level confronted my Indian pupils with a test designed for middle-class seventh-graders. For the two girls taking the test, it was little more than another experience in school frustration. The publishers of the test are aware of this problem and recommend that for low socioeconomic pupils the level of the test administered is better suited for grades eight through ten. Nevertheless, the test was distributed to seventh-graders in all Indian schools. Completed test booklets were mailed to Vancouver. Results of the test were never sent back to the village. I obtained the results six months after the testing.

Norma tested an overall IQ of 83, one IQ point higher than she had tested in the seventh-grade program on a different test the year before. She placed with a numerical equivalent of "1," the bottom group. In a provincial high school she would consequently have been counseled into a terminal occupational course. Dorothy tested an overall IQ of 92, attaining a numerical equivalent of "2" which would have precluded any alternative except a terminal occupational course for her as well. The mean IQ of all day school pupils for the test was 85.8; for residential school pupils the mean IQ was 88.2. The mean of Dorothy's and Norma's scores was 88. In the various subject areas of the Lorge-Thorndike test the mean score of residential school pupils was higher than that of day school pupils in every subject.

In addition to the province-wide use of standardized tests for seventh graders, the local superintendent of the provincial schools distributed copies of the grade VII examinations for June 1963, to Indian day schools. Administration of the tests was required in provincial schools, but teachers in Branch schools were advised they could use the tests as they pleased. Since the testing program seemed to give some special status to the girls and seemed to link the village school with other school programs, I did administer several parts of the test. Described in a cover letter as "searching and comprehensive," the tests focused on minute details of the pre-scribed provincial curriculum quite unrelated to what had been accomplished at the village during the year. For example:

> Long John's treacherous plan for getting the treasure was
> discovered by ——— while hiding in ———.

A group intelligence test was administered to the entire class in May 1963. For most of the young children, and possibly for some of the older ones whose school-ing had all been at the village, this test was the first experience of its kind. The test used was the California Test of Mental Maturity, or CTMM, Short Form, 1957 edition, Primary Level, a test which requires no reading ability. The highest total mental age score attained among the pupils was equivalent to a mental age of elev-en years. The test identifies a language and nonlanguage IQ. The range of nonlan-guage IQ's recorded was from 51 to 107. Two of the youngest children failed to make sufficient responses on the language section of the test to be measured; one pupil made no mark anywhere on the test except for printing her name. The range of IQ scores for the total test was from 46 to 100.

Ranking the children by total scores showed a tendency for the IQ scores of the children from each household to cluster. This observation was put to test and re-vealed a statistically significant difference (.05 level) between mean IQ's for chil-dren from different families. Ranking the families according to the mean of the IQ scores achieved by their school-age children also corresponds with the way I would rank the same families from less- to more-acculturated as mean scores rise.

Reggie and his cousin had the highest mean IQ score. Dorothy and her brother were next in order, followed by the mean IQ scores for the two school children from Norma's household and then by Walter and his brothers.

This difference between mean "family IQ's" also corresponds to family size. Children from smaller families generally performed better on the test. Children whose test scores were in the upper third of the class group included one child being raised as an only child, one family in which there were only two offspring, and three children of ordinal positions either first or last for which they received special attention (e.g., oldest child and only son, or baby sister among siblings up to twenty years older). Children who tested in the lower two-thirds of the group were from families in which from four to ten children of school age or younger resided in one household.

The manual accompanying the Primary Level of the CTMM describes how the test can be used both for a readiness prediction for grade one and for an appraisal of grade placement (that is, a mental age converted to a grade equivalent). The scores of the twelve pupils with the lowest raw scores were compared with predictions for first grade success, after the adjustment of scores for advanced ages and for spring testing. The prediction for two children in their third year at school was "Usually will have difficulty—more readiness desirable." Six children were in the category "Can do first grade work." Of these six pupils only one was a beginner in school; the oldest of the six was attending for his fifth year. Four children had scores which fell within the predictive range described as "Should do well in grade one." One of these four children was Reggie, the youngest pupil but also the pupil whose raw score for his age gave him the highest IQ score (100) achieved on the test. It was predicted that three other children of chronological ages 11+, 12+, and 15 would be able to "do well in grade one." The fifteen-year-old was in school for his eighth year; he was reading at the upper second-grade level. The three other children were struggling with the last of the grade-one readers, possibly for their fourth or fifth consecutive year.

Various levels of the CTMM tests are described as overlapping with the level next above or below and therefore the adjacent series is suitable for retesting. The next higher level of the test was used a few days later among all older pupils who could take a test requiring reading ability. The retest resulted in a mean IQ gain of + 14 points and a range of IQ changes from 5 to 29 IQ points higher!

The Wechsler Intelligence Scale for Children, or WISC, was administered to twenty-two pupils as an individual test. With only one exception, children again scored higher on performance skills, ranging from 4 to 35 points higher in performance over verbal IQ. The manipulation of blocks and puzzles on two of the performance subtests was intriguing to most of the children. No village child had ever experienced this type of test.

TABLE 2

COMPARISON OF WISC AND CTMM SCORES OF TWENTY-ONE VILLAGE PUPILS,
MAY 1963

	Name of Test	Performance or Nonlanguage IQ	Verbal or Language IQ	Full Scale or Total IQ
Range	WISC	65–104	45–96	50–98
Median		86	67	74
Range	CTMM	51–107	[a]-90	46–100
Median		71	60	66

[a] Low raw scores for two pupils yielded no measure of language IQ.

Table 2 presents a comparison between scores on the WISC and the CTMM for twenty-one pupils in class. The median IQ is given to eliminate the influence of spuriously low scores. In both tests nonverbal IQ's are higher than verbal scores. The range of scores on the WISC is not as great as on the CTMM.

The Educational Testing Service's School and College Ability Test battery

(SCAT), an aptitude test, was administered to upper-grade pupils. Results of these tests are given in percentile bands and are not directly comparable to IQ score results. The test level used, developed for typical students in grades 4, 5, and 6, proved very difficult for all but the most capable of the older pupils. Many scores were in the spurious range. On the SCAT test a distinction is made between verbal and quantitative components of the test. All quantitative scores for the children who completed the test exceeded the verbal scores. Percentile bands did not overlap on any scores.

The most consistent finding from results of the three tests, the CTMM, WISC, and SCAT, is the greater score achieved on what is variously termed the "nonlanguage," "performance," or "quantitative" part of the battery. For both the CTMM and WISC scores, in twenty out of twenty-one pairs of test results pupils made better scores on the nonlanguage parts of the test. The SCAT results lend further support to this finding; all five pupils who scored above spurious ranges on subtests performed better on the nonverbal tests.

Among several other standardized achievement tests administered to the older pupils was a test purported to appraise listening as a skill. Although this listening test was read to the pupils it seemed to depend more on verbal comprehension than on any special skills of listening. The test provided no new insight to the problem of nonlistening among the pupils.

In routine classroom testing, spelling was the most often tested subject. Lists of spelling words lend themselves to the short tests that were expected by the older pupils, although when lists were too long or difficult there were attempts at cheating. The four oldest pupils did their spelling at grade level and preferred to do so in spite of not being able to recognize many of the words they learned and not being able to pronounce some of them. Use of the twenty-word Phonovisual Diagnostic Test at the beginning and end of the year with seven boys showed little improvement in the number of words spelled correctly. Three boys still could not spell any of the words on the list, while the others gained two or three words. However, all the boys were able to identify more component parts of words at the end of the year, presumably a consequence of some instruction in phonics. Only two boys of the group could identify the "sh" sound in the word "shape." Such a sound is lacking in the pronunciation of English among most villagers, reflecting the absence of that sound in Kwakwala.

Aside from giving regular spelling tests, I did not make wide use of subject tests. In a sense every assignment and every problem was a test, but at the same time neither the pupils nor I needed a constant formal reminder of their special difficulties in arithmetic computation or of their problems in reading comprehension and vocabulary. At times I let children proceed at their own pace through workbooks or texts, attempting to help them individually as they required it. The assignments were quite uneven in difficulty, however, and pupils often sat for long periods of time waiting for the teacher's help. Because of the extensive mutual help in which pupils so frequently engaged, I had to remain with the same pupils to insist on individual work if I wanted an indication of how well each of them had understood an explanation and assignment dealing with unfamiliar materials.

VILLAGE CHILDREN AS PUPILS: SOME CASE STUDIES

Even a description of only one classroom or of a group such as "the older pupils" masks much individual behavior. This section gives a description of the classroom with specific emphasis on the children who have been the focus of this study. The study concludes with an epilogue describing subsequent changes in formal education for village pupils and reporting how these same pupils have fared in a variety of new settings.

Joseph   For 15-year-old Joseph, school played a minor role during the year. Two years earlier, as a fifth grader, he had attended school for 173 days and had been promoted with the comment, "Capable of good efforts." The following year, his record showed thirty-two days total attendance; "Stopped Jan. 15" was the only entry recorded in the school register. During my year as teacher Joseph came to school a total of fourteen days. In November he left school to dig clams. At our next few encounters he informed me he thought he might come back to school, and then he made no further mention of it.

Not until the following summer when he drafted his request to the superintendent did he again express interest in returning to school. He had borne the idleness of spring in anticipation of a fishing job for summer. When he did not get a position on a crew, going away to school represented the only other possibility for getting away from the village. However, there was no school opportunity available for him. He did not even consider returning to the village classroom the following year to join five of his younger brothers and sisters, the youngest nine years his junior. He still clung to his dream of leaving the village and going away to school, but there was no official encouragement for his hope.

Norma   Except for the few weeks in the fall when Joseph and his age-mate were in class, and an even shorter time when an eighth-grade girl attended, Norma and Dorothy were the two senior pupils in the school. As far as the rest of the children were concerned, the two girls dominated the class. Only on rare occasions were they divided in their companionship, but such days were difficult ones for the children and for the teacher as well. Although they are separated by only a year in age, the girls are also separated by a generation, and in their attitudes toward school the difference in generation is evident.

Particularly as the summer approached, Norma complained that school was becoming increasingly boring and increasingly a place where the activities seemed more appropriate for little children than for her. The frustration she encountered in doing her assignments, particularly in arithmetic, further increased her discontent.

During the previous year Norma had been chased out of school in January. This is the version that the teacher put in the school record:

Suspension
Larry Duncan   Frances Willie   Norma Hawkins
    On Thursday afternoon of Jan 11th these children were given a Language assignment. This they began, the classroom being normally quiet. At about 2

pm. for no apparent reason these three students proceeded to play "tag" and ran wildly about the class. After several requests to stop this teacher finally caught Larry Duncan by the arm and the three were sent home. After talks with the 3 students on morning of Jan 12th they were given indefinite suspensions.

Here is Norma's account of the event and what followed:

One day Joseph Willie, Frances Willie, Larry Duncan, and I were playing tag in class. And the teacher chased us out. I try to come back Monday. But he chased me out again. So I stayed out of school for awhile. Then I went to another village. But I stopped around middle of June. Cause everybody was talking about me. Walking around 2 oclock in the morning. I didn't like it.

Until she reached grade seven, Norma's attendance and promotions at the village school had been regular. Possibly to help balance the number of pupils between a husband and wife team, Norma even had skipped one grade so she could be transferred to the senior room. Like most students, she had repeated grade one, but she had not repeated any other grade.

Norma spent three years moving from grade seven to grade eight. The first year she transferred to St. Michael's during the year. At the beginning of the following year she reported to the village school and was again assigned to grade seven. It was during this year that she was expelled and later attended the day school in the neighboring village. She was in attendance there during the annual spring testing, although she did not remain in school through the end of the term. During my year as teacher she completed grade seven and began to do grade eight work. She understood that she would continue in grade eight the year following, as she could not complete the grade starting in midyear as she had done.

Since a teacher at a neighboring village had information regarding test performance and classroom achievement, I wrote asking him for his appraisal and his recommendation on her future education. The test results showed that Norma had placed in the bottom 4 percent on a scholastic aptitude test, and the teacher's note of explanation included the following:

Indeed, I had Norma in my school last year. She was expelled at your village. About a month before the end of the school year she disappeared. . . . Personally speaking, I don't think you should recommend her. Maybe you could wait till you have marked the district Grade VII exams. Then you will have a very good idea of how she's doing!! (Don't cry!!)
If you still think it over to recommend her [for high school] then talk it over with the district superintendent when he comes (about February). Since the austerity policy, I don't think they will spend any money for that purpose.

In class Norma worked independently most of the time. Instead of asking for help, she customarily skipped over difficult problems in arithmetic and reading. The work she completed on her own revealed that often she had not understood the concepts or vocabulary of the material. A science text with a word list and blanks to be filled in at the end of each chapter resulted in responses like "Sailing ships depend on moving masses of *windmills,*" or "Air which is squeezed into a small space is said to be *breathing.*" Although she read many library books of her own choosing during the year, I was never able to convince her that reading books which she enjoyed was a preferable alternative to "doing reading" which to her meant sitting at her desk staring into space while a reader and accompanying workbook whose vocabularies were almost infinitely beyond her remained open but ignored.

An earlier teacher observed of her, "Capable, must be encouraged and prodded." Prodding no longer seemed appropriate for the young lady she had become, but it was possible to encourage her through recognition of her progress in spelling, through her skill in arithmetic computation, and through her efforts at the independent reading assignments in her texts. Although she did bully younger children at times, her demeanor was more often that of a young woman than of a child. Her out-of-school activities ran a wide range: she often took care of her household and the children in it, participated in the drinking parties with older teen-agers and young adults, and occasionally still joined in the play and activities of the children. Her growing interest in boys and the fact that "there's lots more kids" at Alert Bay increased her interest in attending school there. The boy-interest was subject to whims. At the very end of school she wrote:

> I'm not interested in boys. There to nuisance. And they make trouble for girls sometimes. And I don't believe in going steady.

Confronted with grade-eight work in the provincial school at Alert Bay during the following year, Norma suggested in this comment her perception of herself as a student:

> We high school kids are having a Exam tomorrow till Friday. I hope I pass. But I doubt it. I'm very stupid in school. We get French. And the math is different from last year.

Dorothy and her brother   Dorothy almost consistently out-performed Norma in class, a situation of which she was either unaware or which she did not wish to acknowledge. Her IQ test results on several tests ranged between 90 and 100, with nonverbal scores typically higher by a few points than her scores on the verbal IQ. Math was her best and favorite subject, and on one standardized test her quantitative score placed her in the 66–85th percentile range for seventh graders.

In spite of close family ties, constant companionship, and similar ages, there were differences in the commitment of the two girls toward their schoolwork which reflected a different orientation toward school in their respective households. Dorothy's mother, one of Norma's older sisters, attended school only briefly; she decries the fact that she cannot read or write and she refers to herself as "stupid." Dorothy's father completed grade eight at St. Michael's. He enjoys reading, writes well, and converses easily in English. Both of Dorothy's parents encouraged their two children in school. Distinctions were made in their home between school nights and nonschool nights for bedtime and between household duties on school and nonschool days. "Mom always does the dishes on school days but I do them on weekends."

Dorothy's mother was the only parent to ask for the teacher's help in trying to enroll children at St. Michael's for the following year. She wanted both Dorothy and Norma to continue their education at Alert Bay. Most of Dorothy's previous schooling had been at St. Michael's. Curiously, in spite of letters sent to enroll the girls at St. Michael's the preceding February, and of the enrollment being a virtual fact by May, no place had been held at the residence for the girls. If the teacher had not been available at the end of the summer to help insure their enrollment at St. Michael's, it is questionable whether the girls could have attended school anywhere except back at the village where they would have repeated another final year.

As a team Dorothy and Norma exhibited an intangible kind of reluctance toward the teacher at the same time they pursued their routine classwork. They seldom offered to help in class and were rather likely to refuse any direct request to do so. They seemed to maintain a distinction between their physical presence in class and any control over their wills which the teacher might exercise. As the year progressed, some ill feeling between the teacher and Norma's family arose because of an incident not directly related to the classroom, and the reluctance of the girls as pupils seemed to increase as a result. The aura of the classroom became more negative. Under the influence of the older children this negative and subtlely hostile feeling pervaded the classroom. In the face of almost any kind of classroom ultimatum, the teacher stood alone with the pupils lined up behind their older spokesmen. The younger children were quickly socialized to this system; its impact on six-year-old Reggie is discussed later.

Dorothy's brother had spent most of his school years at St. Michael's just as Dorothy had. The two children had gone fishing with their parents every summer, and as a result neither had spent much time in the village. The boy seemed glad to return to school in the fall. Initially he showed a strong attachment for the teacher and he often remained after school to help in the classroom. He was a frequent visitor at the teacherage as well. His close identification eventually gave way to the stress of the climate within the class. He stopped helping after school and he became less cooperative in the classroom. By the end of the school year he was performing minimally and with reluctance. Although he never participated fully with his peers in their most rigorous or daring activities (like sucking gas or vandalizing vacant houses), he joined them more and more frequently. His parents were distressed to watch him become "like the other kids here," but his father cautioned his mother that anything she said "would only make it worse."

In showing me his fifth-grade report card from St. Michael's, Dorothy's brother explained that the report contained "the lowest grades you can get and still pass." However, his work was far ahead of the several boys in grade five in the village school. He was promoted during the year to grade six and began working in several books at that grade level. His erratic classroom behavior and scholastic performance were matched by his test performance results. His performance IQ on the WISC was 104, 33 IQ points above his verbal score, yet on the CTMM he was the only pupil whose language score exceeded his nonlanguage score (language IQ: 79, nonlanguage IQ: 71). His grade placement scores from three previous years of testing at St. Michael's, presented in Table 3, compare his age and grade in school with his test grade placement over a four-year period. His performance in the upper elementary grades is characteristic of the "falling off" of academic achieve-

TABLE 3

ACTUAL GRADE IN SCHOOL AND TEST GRADE PLACEMENT FOR ONE VILLAGE
PUPIL FOR FOUR CONSECUTIVE YEARS

Actual Grade at Time of Testing	Test Grade Placement
3.8	3.6
4.8	4.1
5.8	5.0
6.8	5.0[a]

[a] Based on a different test battery from three previous years.

ment in each successive grade that has been reported for Indian pupils in the United States (Coombs *et al.* 1958:35). Scattered results of previous tests administered at the school lend additional evidence to this achievement pattern, although complete longitudinal data were not available for any other pupil in the school.

A teacher who taught Dorothy's brother at the day school in Alert Bay remembered him as "lazy but likeable, low in arithmetic and sloppy in handwriting." Her most favorable impressions were of his singing and art. She felt that he had a good sense of color combinations but that his work generally was copied rather than original. (In the village school he was the only older boy who did not draw Indian designs.) I asked his teacher if she had passed him at the end of his year. "Conditionally," she replied. "We are forced to push them on."

Recalling his deportment in class, this teacher reported Dorothy's brother as being "a little saucy." She recalled his resentment at being corrected in front of the other children: "If I corrected him, he'd cry so sometimes. They said that he was the apple of his parent's heart and that if he was clamped down on he'd resent it."

The parents talked about sending the two children to St. Michael's for the following year, but as the opening of school drew nearer they decided against having them both away. Since Dorothy had to leave home to continue her education, her brother remained with his parents at the village.

Walter   Twelve-year-old Walter was one of eight older boys who constituted an intermediate age and ability group in the class. Like most other boys in this group Walter had progressed steadily through the lower grades after the inevitable repetition of the first year. He "tried hard" in school and was the most diligent of the male pupils, although he either stopped any school task instantly if he could not cope with it or he skipped around in his texts and workbooks to find pages that looked easy or interesting. An entry from my journal late in the school year describes a pattern he often followed in class:

> Walter often gets "stuck" at the beginning of reading and just sits there waiting for me to happen by. Equally as often he waits until the moment when I start to help another group and then he comes to ask for help. This brings on my anger, his reaction (often with a mumble like "Fuck you" under his breath) and, later in the morning a story written to me: "Mr. Harry Wolcott, why were you mat at me for?"

Upon completing an assignment or an entry in his writing book he usually presented it immediately to the teacher like a personal gift.

In spite of his diligence, Walter shared with the older pupils the tendency toward reluctance and sullenness in class. He followed a pattern common to most of
the older boys of making timely and prolonged visits to the school toilet. At the beginning of the school year I was shocked to hear that past teachers had been known
to lock the toilets. By the middle of the year I was surprised at how little distress I
felt when the vagaries of the village water supply necessitated my locking them. I
was sure that far fewer children would request to go home during class than ever
requested to use the toilet at school. No completely humane and satisfactory scheme
for prorating the use of the school toilet was devised during the year or was described by teachers at the other village schools. Walter's flexibility in maximizing
the time and opportunity for using the school toilet in spite of constantly changing
rules and procedures was remarkable.

Occasionally Walter requested schoolwork to take home. He so impressed his
mother with his dedication to school that she promised he could attend St. Michael's the following year, although she made no official application for him. Walter was delighted with the prospect of going to a different school, for this was his
sixth consecutive year at the village school.

Walter had another reason for wishing to go away to school. He was the victim
of much taunting from an older brother and from another older boy in class and he
longed to escape their subjugation of him. On one weekend he and an age-mate
incurred the special wrath of the two older boys. Walter was warned that he was
"going to get it" at school. He was so concerned about the threat he left the village
for the weekend and stayed away through the following Monday. When he returned to school on Tuesday he and his age-mate "got it" just as the older boys
had warned. Later that day he wrote out his feelings in class:

> Dear Mr. Wolcott. How are you? I feel bad myself. I wouldn't like to be
> here. I wouldn't like to come to school here. Not for long. Just for somebody
> anyways. They like to beat me up. So that's not the way. What I feel sorry
> about is what they did to me and Leslie. I just didn't like it, Mr. Wolcott. My
> sister told me not to stay here. Not in this old place. Me and Leslie. No use of
> me and Leslie staying here.

I have taken editorial liberties with Walter's entries. Here is the above para-
graph exactly as he wrote it:

> Dear mr Walcott How are you I feel bad myslaf I woulding like to be Here
> I woulding like to come school here not for long just for somebody anyways
> thay like to bed me up so that not the why what I feel sorry about that what
> did to me and Lislie I just diding like it mr. Walcott my sister told me not stey
> Here not in this old please me and Lislie no yous of me Lislie steying Here.

Reggie   When six-year-old Reggie entered the Blackfish Indian Day School in
midyear he brought an educational background different from all the other pupils.
Although he had started school only the previous September, Reggie had been attending a provincial school. Reggie was no stranger to the village, but his parents
had never intended for him to attend school there. When exigencies made a return

to the village their only alternative, they endeavored to have Reggie miss as little school as possible. On his first morning in the village he was ready and waiting when the school bell rang, an official transfer and his previous report card clasped in his hand. Reggie's father came out of the house to introduce himself and to explain that the family would be living at the village for a while.

Reggie's report card from his teacher at the provincial school showed all "C's" and included the comment that Reggie certainly liked physical education. If teachers have covert ways of communicating, such a report card can be interpreted to describe Reggie as a very average pupil—or less. But among his village classmates, Reggie was not very average at all. He was eager and responsive from the moment he entered the classroom that first morning. He had progressed farther in reading in his first six months than some of the village children had in as many years. The note from his previous teacher said that he was reading in *Dick and Jane,* page 10. He was tentatively placed with a group of village pupils reading the same book but farther along in it. That group included two fourth-graders, a third-grader, and two of the best-performing second grade children. The youngest pupil in the group was three years Reggie's senior.

The class was intrigued with what Reggie could do, and for his first hour and a half in class he was the star performer in volunteering answers and in exemplifying classroom courtesy. He asked many questions about what he was to do in class. Fascinated as they were, the older pupils had no intention of letting this new little boy perform so well. Before the first morning was over Reggie reported that one of the oldest boys had threatened to slap his face. Reggie quickly learned to keep such threats to himself, and even to hide the tears as best he could when the threats became a reality. By noon he informed me, "I won't be here tomorrow. I'm going to school at Port Hardy." His father had told me that very morning that the family might stay as long as two years.

Most of the characteristics that made Reggie a refreshing addition to the class gradually disappeared. He began to perform less well, to work very slowly, to volunteer fewer answers to teacher questions, and to confront school tasks with increasing reluctance. After a few days he refused to participate in a class activity, and the teacher sent Reggie home with a note about it, counting on home support. Reggie returned shortly with a note which explained his refusal but assured the teacher that he would cooperate in the future. Reggie added, "Or I'll get a spanking."

Reggie was caught between the positive and achievement-oriented attitudes of his parents (and teacher) and the negative, nonacademic orientation of his peers. He seemed to minimize the conflict with his peers by minimizing his achievement at classroom tasks, particularly when the achievement was in relation to and subject to the scrutiny of his classmates. When he could work independently on activities which the other children could not judge he performed better, whereas in a group he sometimes became the least efficient pupil. On both the CTMM and the WISC he tested the highest total IQ of any pupil, with total IQ scores of 100 and 98 on the two tests. On the WISC test his performance IQ of 100 exceeded his verbal IQ by 4 points.

Reggie's parents made the most frequent inquiries of any parents about their son's schoolwork. They were concerned with his behavior change and his growing aloofness to classroom tasks. They spoke often of their regret that they had been unable to let Reggie stay in the provincial school where they felt he had been doing so well and getting a "good start." They were particularly worried about his reading, and his mother offered to help him at home by letting him reread his stories to her. It was agreed that Reggie could take his reading book home in the afternoon, but he rarely did. One day his cousin appeared back at school in the late afternoon to get Reggie's reader. He explained that Reggie was "supposed" to bring the book home but "he didn't want to because those kids always tease him."

Although Reggie's behavior in class during the spring conformed increasingly to the typical behavior pattern among the pupils, life in class was never completely resolved for him. He was threatened constantly. Unlike most other pupils Reggie had no slightly older siblings or cousins in the class or in the village on whom he could depend for help and support in his defense. His parents warned him against making the older children angry and comforted him with the promise that next year he could go to a different school.

EPILOGUE

Toward the end of spring a decision had to be made about whether to open school at the village the following year. The range of attitudes of villagers toward the day school had been relayed to the regional superintendent, and he visited the village to discuss the problem. The superintendent asked the chief councillor's opinions about the alternatives for school. The chief explained why at least for Blackfish Village he felt that it was better to send children to a residential school, and he supported his position by reviewing the merits of residential schooling and the problems of the village school. The superintendent explained Branch policy, stating the case for day schools and for parent responsibility. As he rationalized official policy point by point he paused to ask the chief, "Now what do you think?"

"I just told you," came the inevitable reply.

Finally the superintendent asked the crucial question, "Do you want me to close the Blackfish Indian Day School next year?"

Confronted by such an approach, the chief deliberated on his response. "I don't know what the others would want." He paused again and then concluded, "So I guess we better have it." Perhaps he was not convinced that his opinion mattered anyway, for during the discussion he said at one point, "If you gonna close the school, you gonna close it, no matter what you tell me here. You can do whatever you want."

If the village school was to remain open, the superintendent wanted to know if there were any special problems with which he could help. The chief expressed concern about the older boys in class, that they were "spoiling it for the little ones." The superintendent said he would try to arrange places at St. Michael's for the older boys. Regardless of good intentions, the parents of the children involved were neither consulted about the decision nor informed that a decision had been made. During the latter part of the summer, parents were notified that certain pupils were to attend St. Michael's, including most of the older male pupils. No villager understood exactly how certain pupils but not others were selected to attend the residential school.

When the Blackfish Indian Day School opened in the fall of 1963, sixteen pupils enrolled. Four children, including Dorothy's brother and Walter, were assigned to the sixth grade and were the oldest pupils. During the year six children entered as beginners.

Staffing was a great problem during the year. The isolation of village life aggravated already existing family problems for the first teacher, and after six weeks he requested a two-week leave. In his absence a substitute teacher was sent to the village. The teacher's family situation was not resolved, and at Christmas he resigned. Another person was sent to the village after the first of the year. His reaction to the capacity of his pupils was a typical one of surprise at their low abilities:

> In my opinion it was a fallacy to attempt to work at their paper grade level. I dropped Grades #6 #5 #4 to a total grade 4 level. All others to grade 1.

Since almost half the village children had attended other schools during the year anyway, an official decision was made in the summer of 1964 to close the village school. This time there were no meetings between villagers and Branch officials. Rumors about closing the school were confirmed as the agent began contacting parents to make arrangements for sending children to St. Michael's. The closing was described as temporary. During the year all books, furnishings, and supplies were removed from the teacherage and classrooms, and every door and window of the Blackfish Indian Day School was boarded and nailed. That is the way the school stands today.

Closing the school had consequences far beyond the walls of the classroom. The school had served not only as an educational institution but also as an official recognition of the band, formally linking the village with the rest of contemporary Canadian society. Closing the school had the effect of withdrawing this recognition, somewhat akin to closing an embassy and recalling the ambassador. The school bell in September 1964, played a Pied Piper's tune that called all the school-age children away from the village. Families who did not want their children sent away had to move to other villages or to Alert Bay, and the moving of some families precipitated the moving of others. Two years after the closing of school only two village households, Walter's and Joseph's, were still being maintained all year. Families from five other households returned periodically to their village homes but left them locked and boarded for increasingly longer periods.

While the speed of the impact of the closing the school may not have been anticipated, the consequences were viewed by many as either the best alternative for the village or at least the inevitable one. There has been talk favoring an amalgamation of all local bands, an idea that receives strong support from officials of the Indian Affairs Branch. Any action which encourages people to leave the outlying villages and move to more concentrated centers of the Indian population is a step in this direction. Other villagers see no way of making any changes that would restore the band to its former status among the bands. Villagers who left Blackfish Reserve years before wonder how fellow bandsmen have held out so long in the anachronism of village life. One former villager said of the few people still remaining at Blackfish, "I guess the people left there are mostly clam diggers."

The time which has elapsed since the initial fieldwork in 1962–1963 has made it possible to follow the progress of the pupils as they have continued in school. Two observations are possible now that would not have been possible without some elapsed time between the initial fieldwork and this writing. First, every village child who was a pupil in the day school during the school year 1962–1963 was subsequently retained at a grade level at least once during the next three years. Second, in watching the children progress through the grades the behavior patterns that seemed related to individual personality at one point begin to look more like age-graded stages as one watches children pass through them. Each of the pupils studied has, in the three elapsed years, taken on some of the characteristics and attitudes of the group of pupils who were next older during the year of the study.

Joseph's situation had changed least of all except that he spent more time at Alert Bay and his escapades included an occasional foray to the beer parlor. He had not entirely given up hope of going away to school. He received application forms in the summer of 1965 for a special course the Branch considered offering the following February, although this possibility seemed remote to him and a wait of a half year looked more like an official stall than a promise of action. An increase in the price per box of clams for the 1965–1966 season offered more immediate rewards.

Norma attended the provincial school in grade eight "occupational" the year after the study. She and Dorothy lived at St. Michael's. The following year she attended eighth grade in a provincial school near Vancouver where she boarded with a non-Indian family. She still considered school a boring place:

> I'm just fine, just a little lonely for my family. I like it here all right. Yes, I am still going to school, kind of boring now.

In March she quit school. She decided that she would not return to school again if it necessitated being isolated from her family and her own people. The following September she was in Vancouver with her mother, but she did not enroll in school.

Dorothy completed grade eight at Alert Bay and, like Norma, went on the following year to board with a White family and attend grade nine in a provincial school near Vancouver. She contrasted herself with Norma: "She thinks school is boring, but I think it's lots of fun." Once during the year she changed schools and families: "I didn't like it over there." Her interest in school wavered at times but she still considered an education necessary for her future:

> As for the little girl who used to love Math, she's fine I guess, except now things have changed. I don't like Math so much now, it's not so easy as it used to be. Sometimes I feel like quitting school, I feel like giving up, I feel like chickening out in other words. . . . I want to be everything, teacher, nurse, and a policewoman, but I guess I'll be a nurse then I'll only have to go to school one more year and I'll be seventeen by then, gosh, getting old.

Her enthusiasm diminished rapidly when she was not passed to grade ten. Faced with the prospect of repeating grade nine, the loneliness of the past year loomed more formidable. She spoke of returning to school someplace where she and Norma could stay with her mother or grandmother—but when school started the following September she returned with her parents to the village instead.

Now it was Dorothy's brother who felt the importance of school in the final throes of his formal education. As one of the oldest pupils at the village school he completed his sixth-grade work. He enrolled in St. Michael's the following year as a seventh-grader:

> I sure feel funny a big boy like me in grade seven and my sis in grade nine. But I never stop school 'til I don't know grade 11 or something like that.

The following summer he rented a company gill-net boat and, with the guidance of his father, made a good season of summer fishing. By the time he "pulled up his net" to return to school he had earned money for school clothes and for personal expenses, and he followed in his sister's footsteps to live near Vancouver and attend a provincial school.

Walter had hoped to go to St. Michael's in order to escape the taunting of older boys in the village. When the older boys were sent away to St. Michael's, Walter had a good year in the village as a sixth-grader during the last year of the village school. With the taunting eliminated, Walter discovered that he did not wish ever to go away to school. "I just don't want to leave my parents, that's all," he explained. When the school was closed, however, there was no choice for him but to leave his family and go to St. Michael's.

Walter repeated grade six the following year. His effort in school was duly noted by his teacher at Alert Bay who commented, "If he gets something he likes, he's heads down and hard at it," a reputation he was gaining for his prowess on the playing field, for his perseverance (but not necessarily for his performance) in schoolwork, and for his summer work on the seine crew.

Like Walter, most village children now live at St. Michael's during the school months and attend the Indian Day School at Alert Bay. In some families the thought of separating a child from the household is disturbing to parents and offspring. If the children express concern about attending the school or are unhappy once they arrive, then their parents become distressed also. One parent reported how her child cried during her first week at St. Michael's. "She must be so don't like it," the mother explained, and her worry caused her to consider moving to Alert Bay so the child would not have to live at the residence. In other cases children and parents alike are happy when the children return to St. Michael's after the summer holiday. From the larger families so many children (up to six) attend St. Mike's that the preschool children who must remain at home are the ones who find themselves separated from their sibling companions.

In every family which sends children to St. Michael's the preparation for school marks a special occasion. Most children receive a scrubbing at home before going off to school. If new school clothes have not been purchased earlier they are purchased just before the children register. The trip to Alert Bay from the village is a family affair, although most of the family remain behind while one parent or an older sibling actually conducts the children to the office at the residence. Some villagers note of others, "As soon as they get the children in school, off they go the the beer parlor."

Most village children still attend schools operated by the Indian Affairs Branch. However, Reggie's family and two other families have moved to White communities so that their school-age children can live at home and attend provincial schools. The effort of Reggie's parents to get a good education for their children has dominated their decisions. When a poor fishing season in the summer of 1963 did not improve their financial position, they saw only one alternative. Reggie's father took a logging job "up north," one that allowed him steady work but meant separation from his family. Reggie's mother located a place to stay in an urban community on Vancouver Island where the children could attend provincial school. She wrote:

> School is just within walking distance from our place. We were quite lucky to find a spot like this as it was quite hard at first. I came down to find us a house all by myself. But I think my husband will like it here when he sees it. Yesterday we got a TV and the children were really thrilled over it.

In order to maintain a steady income to meet the costs of food and rent and to be able to send their children to the "best kind" of school, Reggie's parents had to be separated from each other and Reggie's mother was left alone in a relatively strange community to run her household apart from her husband, her siblings, and her parents. This was the very situation they had all been trying to avoid.

Occasionally jobs opened up near home and Reggie's father was able to join his family. But he has lost opportunities for steady local work because each summer he has returned to salmon fishing. As his wife explained one autumn:

> He said he wasn't going out this year, and then he quit and went out when it started. I guess it's in his blood.

Quitting any regular job to go fishing for the 1965 season proved to be an unfortunate choice, and Reggie's family had a difficult time financially, a situation that was made more acute by a continual procession of visiting kin enroute to and from Vancouver. "What's to eat? We're really hungry!!" queried an aunt of Reggie's when she and her family arrived after a long day of travel. "So are we," came the unexpected reply. There had been no recent check from Reggie's father.

All the difficulties, the financial worries, the transportation problems, the loneliness of having the family separated and of being the only Indian family in the neighborhood—everything might be worth it to his parents to have Reggie and his younger siblings get their education and do well in school. But school had not gone so well for Reggie.

Village children have rarely been promoted to grade two after only one year in school. Reggie's ability compared to other village children was clearly outstanding. Whether he could do the work of the second grade among urban White pupils was almost impossible to judge at the village school, but he was promoted and he entered provincial school as a second-grader. His second grade teacher noted:

> Reggie's level of work this year has been at a low average for grade 2. When Reggie first came to our class, he appeared very shy and nervous. His written work was of very low standard. He rarely finished any written assignment.

With encouragement and praise Reggie's work habits and written assignments improved to a standard acceptable for grade two.

Reggie was promoted at the end of that year to grade three. On the last day of school in the third grade he was stunned when he received his final report card for grade three with the statement, "Assigned to Grade 3." His mother recounted that he marched straight home, handed the report to her, locked himself in the bathroom, and cried for an hour. He did not respond to her pleading and she became so distraught that she telephoned to ask some of Reggie's playmates to come try to console him. Reggie's mother said that he remained depressed for days, and as the time for starting school drew near again she was still concerned over the meaning of the disappointment to him and to the entire family. Reggie's behavior had led her to wonder about his future: "I thought Reggie was going to be one of those problem kids, but he seems to have come out of it all right." At the same time, she approves his taking education so seriously and she told him he was a good boy for "feeling that way about school."

Communication between school personnel and Reggie's mother is formal and restricted. As one teacher at the provincial school said, "I wish all the parents were as nice as Reggie's mother. She's so eager to help. But still she doesn't interfere with what the teacher is doing." If there is some way that Reggie's mother can assist in her children's formal education, the teachers have not succeeded in making clear to her what it is. Messages from school to home have not been clearly understood. For example, Reggie's mother thought she might help by letting Reggie bring home his reading, but she believed that the teacher did not allow books to be brought home. The teacher said Reggie was allowed to take his books home, but that he did so only when reminded. Reggie's mother said she had no idea Reggie might fail grade three, completely missing a warning in the teacher's written comment on the April report card, "Unless improvement is shown, promotion is doubtful." The following year when a teacher reported that Reggie was doing very well (repeating grade three) his mother wondered hopefully if that meant he might be promoted belatedly to the fourth grade so he could remain with his classmates after all.

Reggie became less inclined to talk about school activities except for his participation in sports, particularly in Little League softball. Only an occasional remark to his mother suggested that his failure in grade three was still on his mind. Reggie made a comment in this regard one day that greatly surprised his mother because, she explained, "we never tell him anything like that." Reggie was pondering aloud the possible reasons for being held back in school. Suddenly he turned to his mother and asked, "I wonder if it's because I'm an Indian?"

Three other one-teacher village schools have been closed since the field study. Children from two of the villages attend provincial schools, and the other children are sent to St. Michael's. In those village day schools still being maintained, the behavior of teachers, pupils, and parents follows persistent and predictable patterns. I had occasion to ask a member of a neighboring village about their new teacher just after the start of another school year. He replied, "Oh, I haven't had a chance to meet that new teacher yet. But I hear he said that the kids in the village are all three years behind in their schoolwork."

7 / In retrospect and prospect

A FUNCTIONAL ASSESSMENT OF EDUCATIONAL NEEDS

IN OUR ZEAL to find ways in which ethnically or socially different people may participate more fully in the dominant society, there is a tendency to extol the virtues of formal education. Even villagers echo the slogan, "Education is the only answer." But education in the terms that villagers think of it is far from "the answer." At a time when the completion of grade ten in British Columbia is a prerequisite for literally any specialized training program and for many jobs, the village child who is encouraged to stay in elementary school to complete an extra year or two because of the advantages of "getting an education" is accepting an educational promise that is more likely to lead to disappointment and frustration than to opportunity. Formal educational programs that are not accompanied by real economic and social opportunities are headstarts to nowhere.

While formal education is not the answer, programs of systematic instruction can provide opportunities and means for meeting some of the problems of acculturation. What can be accomplished and how to proceed depend on answers to questions such as these:

(1) What are the functional needs of villagers which can be met by formal education?

(2) Which of these educational needs can be met through the established system of schools, given whatever limits have been imposed upon teacher effectiveness in terms of resources, personnel, and local acceptance?

(3) What other kinds of educational programs might be developed to meet the needs which the school does not meet?

The dedicated educator should not be called upon singly to assess such a broad spectrum of potential educational activity or to delimit what specific contribution the classroom teacher can make. Educators characteristically assume more responsibility for reform than the educational institution can accommodate, and their very commitment to the efficacy of formal instruction may preclude their ability to recognize its limits. Conversely, because of their culture-bound concepts of what kinds of educational programs are and are not within the domain of the classroom, educators may not always recognize or identify unique opportunities for giving help through education.

It may happen, as evidenced to some extent by the case of Blackfish Village, that the school and teacher are perceived as alien, different, perhaps threatening to the traditional way of life. Under such conditions the best method of developing an effective educational program may be to minimize (but not to eliminate) formal schooling and to avoid linking new opportunities or new programs with the school or teacher. Further, educators must recognize that through the formal curriculum they can transmit elements of the White culture only (Hawthorn *et al.* 1960:312). Because the teacher is willing to take on some added task and because he is already known in the community does not assure that he is the obvious candidate to initiate changes outside the classroom. Where schools have not been accepted by pupils or by the community-at-large it may be well to consider requiring a fewer number of hours in school each day, a shorter school year, and a school calendar more sensitive to local customs. Teachers who discover that their pupils are all "three years behind" are not likely to be the ones to suggest the possibility of requiring less school. However, in working in communities where classroom efforts are essentially thwarted by a hostile climate between pupils and teachers we should investigate how *few* hours or years in class are essential in order for children to make the same educational achievement that reluctant and hostile pupils now make in years and years of compulsory education.

A functional approach to identifying the problems and alternatives relating specifically to the place of schooling for villagers is to ask: What are the needs of villagers which *can* be met by formal education? I suggest below some of the real and immediate needs of villagers relevant to education. There are prior considerations here which demand careful consideration. One crucial question is: Who should make an assessment of educational needs? I have already suggested that the educator himself may be too committed to formal education to make an objective analysis. I feel that during my months as the village teacher I not only lacked perspective, but I am certain that I also lacked time either to identify educational needs beyond immediate classroom expectations or to implement any changes. The kind of assessment needed would require a program of recurring investigations and analyses by research teams whose members represent the perspectives of social scientists as well as schoolmen.

The following are important and immediate needs of villagers which might be met, and, in some cases, are being met by direct educational efforts. Young Blackfish villagers today need: (1) the ability to communicate in English; (2) basic reading, writing, and computational skills; (3) a smattering of "that stuff you learn in school"—partly for the information itself, partly as an experience shared in common with all children in the dominant society—including local, Canadian, and world geography, government and politics, and elementary school science and social studies; (4) familiarity with standard written English and a standard dialect of spoken English; (5) knowledge of how to conduct business in formal meetings (such as those conducted by the agent) ; (6) opportunity to satisfy educational prerequisites for higher grades or special training; (7) knowledge of the use of public transportation and communication facilities; (8) knowledge of an increased range of available leisure-time activities; (9) specific information regarding logging work; (10) knowledge of the nature of the work and the formal prerequisites for certain occupations with which villagers have some contact but about which their information is incomplete, such as teacher, minister, nurse, RCMP, mechanic, clerk, or secretary; (11) health information specific to such problems as to how a too-selective adoption of the White man's diet is related to certain chronic health problems, or of available methods of birth control; (12) instruction in specific skills such as swimming that are related to accident prevention; (13) familiarity with a wider variety of models of drinking behavior in order to establish a precedent for patterns of "social drinking" as alternatives to "going haywire"; and (14) complete and accurate information on Indian rights and benefits, including such specifics as enfranchisement, voting, grievance procedures, welfare rights, and the present legal status of traditional customs like potlatching.

While most of these needs are compatible with classroom activity, teachers may not have much more information than villagers on some of these topics, or the kind of information the teacher has may be at once too superficial and too abstract to be functionally useful. Contrast, for example, the typical social studies unit of the elementary schools on "Lumber, Our Natural Resource," and its conservation and technology themes, with the specific kind of information an Indian boy needs in order to decide whether to seek a logging job—what will be expected of him, how dangerous the work is, how to cope with the constant orders of a White strawboss, or how to get a good name as a logger. As one looks at the list of functional needs it becomes apparent that a major problem is that many of the skills or kinds of knowledge needed by village youths are probably not possessed by the teacher. It would seem that special materials do have to be developed, and that the teacher alone cannot be expected to carry the responsibility for the entire educational program.

Some of the functional needs identified in the list above are already part of the program of the school. Basic literacy is being achieved, the children do gain familiarity with "that stuff you learn in school," and they do share the experience of attending school common to most children in North America. One might well ask why some village pupils succeed so well in classroom tasks when much of the curriculum is so irrelevant in terms of their daily lives and their prior experiences.

One aspect of formal education stands out as the need most compatible with present expectations held for the classroom and most amenable to immediate curriculum improvement—helping children acquire a familiarity with standard written English and a standard dialect of spoken English. There is at present a great deal of interest regarding linguistic approaches to teaching English as a second language. I have not found material that would have been suitable and useful for my pupils, material which would have increased their language proficiency without increasing feelings of inadequacy or self-consciousness about language. If materials presently exist, perhaps in the form of pattern practice for oral English, they should be located, adapted as necessary, and introduced in the classrooms. If materials suitable for the classroom and for teachers untrained in a linguistic approach are not available, efforts to develop them should receive priority wherever educators confront pupils who have a limited background in communicating with or thinking conceptually in the language of instruction.

There is a tendency today for educators to employ the term "cultural deprivation" to explain almost any learning difficulties of groups of children outside the mainstream of society. This term is inadequate and misleading. The case study shows that while children who attend schools may not share the set of cultural assumptions upon which schools are based, the children are not therefore "cultureless." But there are aspects of the school's culture children may lack that greatly increase the distance between teacher and child. Probably the most central of these is a facility with English. The school curriculum is based on assumptions about language competence that cannot be made for all children. Children of different ethnic or social class backgrounds may evidence what can be termed, for the purposes of the school, "linguistic deprivation." Inadequate facility with language is, I believe, a major factor contributing to the lack of school achievement for village pupils, and it is a problem the school can attempt to do something about. I am certain that schools deal inadequately at present with identifying or meeting linguistic deprivation. Because my village pupils wrote so often for me, I feel they made more progress with written English than with oral English. I wish I had been able to help them make greater gains in both.

For any of their educational objectives teachers working in a cross-cultural setting will find increased satisfaction for themselves and a more precise idea of what their pupils are accomplishing if they endeavor to make each of their goals in the classroom specific and discrete. Teachers everywhere typically aspire to goals like "make better readers," "teach an appreciation of great literature and a love of reading books," or "see results in a growth of honesty, kindness, consideration, etc." Such goals lack operational definitions by which teachers or pupils can assess whether the objectives have been attained. At the same time such vaguely defined goals allow teachers to strive toward culturally accepted ideals without specifying the steps through which the learner is expected to acquire the new behaviors. In a community like Blackfish Village which lacks any consensus regarding broadly stated educational objectives, both teacher and pupil have more opportunity to determine what they are attempting to do and whether they have accomplished it when goals are stated in such specific terms as "teach Walter, Tommy, and Leslie how to divide by ten." It is this kind of concreteness that makes subjects like spelling and arithmetic more acceptable to village pupils—they know what is expected, and they can judge how well they have succeeded.

The teachers at local day schools who were able to make their objectives specific were the ones who spoke least disparagingly of their pupils and who occasionally even remarked of classroom success. Teachers who feel successful are likely to have pupils with similar attitudes. As learning increments are defined in smaller and more specific units it is possible for the teacher to use more frequent rewards for academic success. More frequent rewards for correct responses among Blackfish pupils would have been consistent both with village life (pursuing an activity because it is immediately gratifying rather than because one is told to do it) and with psychologically-accepted principles of learning. It is crucial for school people to define specifically what it is they expect to accomplish and to go about their work in such a way that both teachers and pupils have some opportunity for success.

CULTURAL VALUES IN THE CROSS-CULTURAL CLASSROOM

Public education has a strong commitment to imbuing learners with concepts of what is "right." The typical classroom atmosphere is laden with overtones of goodness and badness. The teacher may plunge headfirst into conflict when he attempts to force his own beliefs in a community where values differ from his. However, the classroom does not have to be the battleground for imposed value changes.

The case study provides an illustration of a setting where the teacher was likely to increase community resistance through any attempt to impose his value system on his pupils. No one insists, however, that the teacher impose his values or set himself apart as a judge of right and wrong. The teacher should define the behavior that is acceptable in his classroom, but he is not required to provide standards for the entire community. As Hawthorn has suggested (Hawthorn *et al.* 1960:302), it is better for the teacher to emphasize "individual growth rather than cultural change."

Since the teacher only transmits elements of White culture, he should concentrate his efforts in providing his young pupils with those skills that can be taught in school which will give a child access to opportunities in the dominant society if the child chooses to avail himself of these opportunities. These skills obviously include literacy, standard English, and job information. There are, in addition, certain important "values" held in common by members of the dominant society that can be taught to Indian pupils *as skills rather than as values* so that they will know how to act whenever they engage in formal interactions with middle-class Whites. Important among these skills are the behavioral meanings of punctuality, cleanliness, courtesy, responsibility, respect for property, and dependability in performing tasks. While such attributes are accepted as intrinsically good in a middle-class schoolroom, they can be taught as skills to children who are still too immature to be confronted with whether or not to accept the value system underlying them. In this way the teacher can avoid setting up unnecessary conflict for the child between the family and the school.

At Blackfish Village certain pupils and certain families placed more value on school learning and indicated more acceptance of the teacher and of the way of life he represented than did others. If the teacher can divest himself of a personal need to devote equal energy to each of his pupils, then those children who ask for more help are the pupils toward whom he can direct most of his classroom effort. I only created frustration for myself as the village teacher by attempting to coerce reluctant pupils when I might better have directed my efforts to assisting those few pupils who more frequently asked for my help or attention. I have often wished that I had recognized a greater variety of ways to help and had given more attention to the relatively few pupils who sought my help. For example, after my return home I might have harrassed Branch officials until someone, somewhere in British Columbia found a classroom program suitable for a sixteen-year-old Indian boy who begged to go away to school.

While I suggest that teachers do not need to rely on "intrinsic goodness" in rationalizing their curriculum, and while I suggest that values like "punctuality" or even "cleanliness" can be taught as survival skills for holding jobs or increasing the possibility of acceptance by Whites, I do not think that human values should be excluded from the classroom. The teacher has a value system and life style of his own which he should maintain through the integrity of his own behavior. For all the variation we identify among cultures, each individual can live out but one life style, and, to paraphrase Erik Erikson, for any one individual all human integrity stands or falls with the one style of integrity in which he shares. For the brief duration of his contact, the White teacher is neither required categorically to reject Indian life nor to identify completely with it. The teacher may never fully understand the components of integrity or of love and trust as an Indian or as an individual of any different cultural orientation perceives them, but he does not need to understand other ways of life if he can accept the fact of their existence. It is the integrity of his own life style toward which the teacher should strive as a teacher and as a human being. When a teacher under cross-cultural stress abdicates those aspects of his own way of life that give it integrity he risks becoming as disoriented and goalless as the transitional Indian. The teacher, however, is not faced with the difficult choice between two life styles. If under the stress of immediate and daily contact in the Indian community the teacher can live his life so that it is all right to be a White man, then his pupils may learn through him that it is also all right to be an Indian.

For any child attending school the contact with the teacher provides one of the earliest extended opportunities for what Spindler has referred to as "encounters with cultural agents" (Spindler 1963:380). Except for a fleeting glimpse of the Indian agent or during brief transactions at the store or café, his relationship with his teachers at school may be among the first and among the very few opportunities the village child will ever have for prolonged contact with Whites of a middle-class orientation. School may provide the only opportunity the ethnically different youth will have for a sustained relationship with a White other than on a work crew, in the beer parlor, or in jail. Terms like "acculturation" and "dominant White society" suggest an omnipresence of Whites that is not a characteristic of ethnic enclaves. The classroom is a unique human encounter; of these there are only a finite number for each of us. For the Indian child the experience in the classroom may provide the only time when the distance between the mainstream of the dominant White society and his everyday world is bridged by actual experience.

A breakthrough in my own thinking about formal education at Blackfish Village came about in the metamorphosis of my original research orientation. I had proposed to investigate what it is about village life that makes Indian pupils so refractive to formal education and why Indian pupils fail in school. As I observed and participated in village life and in the classroom, I realized that posing the query in such terms narrowed the perspective of the search. There is another question to ask, one which can be considered an alternative but which is, I think, better regarded as a complement to my original orientation. How do the schools fail their Indian pupils?

Members of the dominant society charged with instructing ethnically-different pupils may recognize that their challenge is not usually stated in terms that imply that the school is also part of the problem in the education of minorities. Such a restatement, however, directs attention to the potential and to the limits within the classroom itself rather than to all the complex problems of acculturation. Instead of placing upon the teacher the responsibility for changing a people's whole way of life, it asks the teacher to focus his effort on his own classroom. Let the teacher consider how he can direct his energy toward specific elements in his instructional program rather than toward making a single-handed attempt at culture change.

References

BENEDICT, R., 1934, *Patterns of Culture*. Boston: Houghton Mifflin Company.

*BOAS, F., 1966, *Kwakiutl Ethnography*. Helen Codere, ed., Chicago: University of Chicago Press.

CODERE, H., 1950, *Fighting with Property: A Study of Kwakiutl Potlatching and Warfare 1792–1930*. New York: American Ethnological Society, Monograph 18.

————, 1961, Kwakiutl, In: *Perspectives in American Indian Culture Change*. Edward H. Spicer, ed., Chicago: University of Chicago Press.

COOMBS, L. MADISON, R. E. KRON, E. G. COLLISTER, and K. E. ANDERSON, 1958, *The Indian Child Goes to School*. Bureau of Indian Affairs, U. S. Department of the Interior.

*DRUCKER, P., 1965, *Cultures of the North Pacific Coast*. San Francisco: Chandler Publishing Company.

*EDUCATION DIVISION, INDIAN AFFAIRS BRANCH, 1965, *The Education of Indian Children in Canada: A Symposium*. Toronto: Ryerson Press.

*FORD, C. S., 1941, *Smoke from Their Fires: The Life of the Kwakiutl Chief*. New Haven: Yale University Press.

HAWTHORN, H. B., C. S. BELSHAW, and S. M. JAMIESON, 1960, *The Indians of British Columbia: A Study of Contemporary Social Adjustment*. Berkeley: University of Calif. Press.

*LAFLESCHE, F., 1963, *The Middle Five: Indian Schoolboys of the Omaha Tribe*. Madison: University of Wisconsin Press.

ROHNER, R. P., 1967, *The People of Gilford: A Contemporary Kwakiutl Village*. Ottawa: National Museum of Canada, Bulletin 225.

SCHMITT, N. and W. S. BARCLAY, 1962, "Accidental Deaths Among West Coast Indians." *Canadian Journal of Public Health*, 53:409–412.

SPINDLER, G. D., 1963, "Personality, Sociocultural System and Education Among the Menomini", In: *Education and Culture: Anthropological Approaches*. G. Spindler, ed., New York: Holt, Rinehart and Winston, Inc.

*———— (ed.), 1963, *Education and Culture: Anthropological Approaches*. New York: Holt, Rinehart and Winston, Inc.

WAX, M. L., R. R. WAX, and R. V. DUMONT, JR., 1964, *Formal Education in an American Indian Community* (with Roselyn Holyrock and Gerald Onefeather). Monograph 1, Society for the Study of Social Problems. Kalamazoo, Mich.: The Society (P.O. Box 190).

---

* Recommended reading.

Afterword, 1989

A KWAKIUTL VILLAGE AND SCHOOL 25 YEARS LATER

"The old Indian ways are just going to die out," my host reflected, adding, with characteristic Kwakiutl panache, "I'm the only one in the family that's even interested in them any more."

For an instant, I was swayed by the familiar lament. I nodded sympathetically, just as I had when I heard essentially that same message of seeming despair a quarter-of-a-century earlier. My thoughts on this hearing were anything but the same, however. During the intervening years I have lived enough of a lifetime to know that things never remain the same: not for a society, not for a community, not for a family, not for any individual. With all honesty, I could nod assent: the old ways are dying out, or, stated less dramatically, are undergoing continual modification.

Those words once heard from Reggie's grandfather were being spoken now by Reggie himself, during the course of a reunion in 1984 after a lapse of many years. My first-grade pupil of 1962 proudly paraded his own young children before me, the eldest "about ready to start school." Self-consciously intent on raising his children as Indian members of contemporary Canadian society ("I'm the only one who married an Indian. My sisters all married white guys"), Reggie himself is the answer today to the same question his grandfather pondered in days gone by: "Who is going to keep Indian ways alive?"

The form in which Reggie lives out and attempts to transmit "his" culture will be less recognizably Kwakiutl than the tradition his grandfather sought to pass on to him. Yet I think that "the Old Man," as we all (and for the most part affectionately) called him 25 years ago, would be pleased to know that Reggie and others of his generation do feel that they have a heritage worth preserving to counterbalance the inevitable forces of change.

"There's no use giving a potlatch anymore," the Old Man had grumbled in the mid-1960s. "The old people don't pay it back, and the young people don't even know what it means! I took him too literally. I believed he really had given up all hope for keeping vestiges of Kwakiutl tradition alive. We both saw evidence during the ensuing years to convince ourselves that Kwakiutl customs in general were headed for the same fate as the Kwakiutl village and school of my study: deteriorated, deserted, and ultimately destroyed. Village Island as residence and the Mamalilikala (or Mamaleleqala) as its residents, a readily identifiable village group among the Kwakiutl people, are gone. Reggie's grandfather, like most old men, and Reggie's grandmother, "the Old Lady," prior to her death a few years before her husband's, mourned the passing of good old days and good old ways and often portrayed themselves as helpless victims of a slow but inevitable extinction of everything Indian.

What a surprise to get a long-distance telephone call in the mid-1970s from one of Reggie's aunts living at the north end of Vancouver Island informing me, "We've been trying and trying to reach you. The Old Man says you better get up here next month. He's giving another big potlatch. He says if you want to see it, you better come now, because this is his third one and it's *definitely* going to be the last!" Three major potlatches given by the very individual who had convinced me the custom was dead! By failing to remain in closer touch, I had failed to realize that the Old Man's resignation to the inevitable demise of Kwakiutl ways was mitigated by a recognition of his own potential to alter that course. Reggie, in turn, represents *his* generation's answer to how to keep Indian ways "alive." They are alive in two ways. First, they remain in living memory. Second, they remain adequately dynamic to provide cultural templates for coping within Canadian society in a manner sufficiently stereotyped to be recognizable as "Indian."

At best, Reggie can maintain only traces of a discernibly *Kwakiutl* life-style. Reggie's father is Indian but not Kwakiutl; he was seldom home and never really "at home" in his father-in-law's family or village. Reggie himself never again stayed as long at the village as he did that year I first met him, the year I served as village teacher. By the end of that year, Reggie's parents had made their more-or-less permanent move back to Vancouver Island, resolved never to return for more than a brief visit. Reggie has lived in the cities and towns of Vancouver Island from its northern tip at rough-hewn Port Hardy to its southern tip at genteel Victoria ever since. He and his wife have a network of immediate kin and casually extended family ties that encompass much of the island.

During the rapid demise of the village precipitated by the closing of its school, Reggie's grandfather moved his household belongings and relocated at Port Hardy. During adolescence, Reggie often stayed with his grandfather, and he regularly joined him during each summer's salmon run until his grandfather finally "hung up his nets for the last time," deciding that with failing vision and failed hearing he was too old to be out fishing. Reggie was in grade 10 at Port Hardy when he quit school and took a job with an auto parts company.

Today, Reggie expresses the same ambivalence about commercial fishing that his father expressed a generation earlier. But, like his father, Reggie seems to "have fishing in his blood." Summer earnings account for the major portion of his annual income, and fishing is the dominant activity in his working and wage-earning life. Qualities that made Reggie something of an anomaly in the village as a six-year-old help him today to negotiate jobs and play his Indianness up or down as social or bureaucratic circumstances demand.

I have lost contact with some village families. What once would have been a relatively easy task through casual conversation or tracing Band Lists readily accessible at the Kwawkewlth Indian Agency at Alert Bay now must be done by locating people in widely dispersed networks, although Port Hardy and "The Bay" have continued to serve as the locus of activity for many of them. The Canadian government provided housing assistance for outlying villagers during efforts at band amalgamation in the mid-1960s, and when several village families relocated along one Alert Bay road someone remarked that it "ought to be nicknamed Little Mamalilikala." But once-critical band and village identities have proven difficult to maintain in the absence of such natural boundary markers as remote locations, not always navigable waters, and villagers not always hospitable to outsiders — even those from neighboring islands. Everyone's name must be on some band list, but precisely which band seems not all that important, especially to younger adults.

The completion of a highway system that now links the northern tip of Vancouver Island with its better-developed southern region has greatly reduced dependency on slow and often unreliable travel by ferryboat. Local travel is easy, but with it has come the paradox that anthropologist Ernestine Friedl describes as lagging emulation: during the same period when outlying villagers were challenged to be "progressive" by relocating at once-thriving Alert Bay, non-Indian residents and many government services formerly housed there were relocating elsewhere on Vancouver Island at nearby Port McNeill and Port Hardy or in the larger island communities of Campbell River, Nanaimo, or Victoria.

Surviving villagers whose offspring attended my classroom are becoming today's new generation of elders. For the most part they are an undistinguished group except for the very fact of their survival in the face of endless stories of personal hardship, "all these years of sickness and sorrow" as one village woman reflected. Accidents and violence continue to account for a large portion of their woes, and alcohol problems are at the root of most of those. Of the roster of pupils in my classroom, fewer than half were still living 25 years later. Those who did survive, however, started families of their own at comparatively young ages. Dorothy found it amusing to think of herself as "a very young grandmother" at age 38.

As in the past, economically successful villagers have "kept the distance" between themselves and other former villagers. They maintain family ties but live apart from Indian ghettoes, self-consciously maintaining middle-class life-styles. They accumulate and display contemporary Western appliances, appurtenances, friends, and often non-Indian spouses as well. Nonetheless, they neither deny their Indian origins nor ignore obligations to participate within and contribute to the larger Indian community.

My impression is that to whatever extent Indian people in Canada continue to be accorded second-class status, less opprobrium attaches to "being Indian" today than 25 years ago. Advantaged by the abundant resources of the region, Indians of the Northwest Coast have always lived within grasp of a relatively prosperous life-style. Official policy and platitudes are not what really matter; the critical element is how Indian people regard themselves and the extent to which they believe they are systematically denied responsibility in, or access to, aspects of mainstream society on the basis of ethnicity. Complaints are still legion, but their impact and significance are diffused, in part because complaining itself is ritualized in the Indian-white dialogue, in part because Indian people have become more vocal about matters that affect them. A new *band directed* elementary school operating in the shadow of St. Mike's in the 1980s, and that includes instruction in Kwakwala in its daily program, is an example of the impact from that growing voice.

REFLECTIONS ON DOING THE STUDY

Not more than a month or two had passed after I completed the doctoral dissertation upon which *A Kwakiutl Village and School* is based when George and Louise Spindler raised the question of how to bring the study before a wider audience. Louise offered the suggestion that not only prompted me to rewrite the dissertation but launched the Spindlers on another major undertaking, editing the Case Studies in Education and Culture.

A Kwakiutl Village and School was one of the four monographs with which the Spindlers introduced the series in 1967. Their original Foreword, "About the Book," has been preserved. (I have updated the section, "About the Author.") That introductory material was part of the format of the new series. Eventually the collection grew to 17 monographs. Although the series never enjoyed the wide distribution of its predecessor, the Case Studies in Cultural Anthropology, many of the titles in the Education and Culture series became well-known and remain so even today.

Contrary to expectations that the more exotic cases, or those in which the influence of formal schooling was new or minimal, would be the most sought after, the monographs that actually "caught on" described settings in North America and circumstances teachers were likely to meet in their own experience. Problems related to poor school performance of young Native Americans fit well with growing concern for Indian education as well as with burgeoning interest in the 1960s and 1970s with problems of minority group education in general.

In spite of aggregate sales of about 20,000 copies and the fact that the original edition remained in print almost 15 years, *A Kwakiutl Village and School* was not considered a commercial success. My royalties started at 19½ cents for copies sold in the U.S. and half that amount for copies sold in Canada. This was my first book, and I was quickly disabused of the notion that authors get rich, although the publication marked a critical step in my academic career. On the other hand, that the study has been well received, is widely known, and continues to be available, now in this Waveland Press version, has been not only rewarding but a bit baffling. I would like to elaborate on this point.

One source of bafflement is that the study appears to be well-known — among educators and anthropologists alike — in spite of the fact that it does not deal at length with the process of ethnographic research. Reflecting customary practice of the day, I paid scant attention to fieldwork procedures in the text, and there are no references on method in the bibliography. Nor were there many references I might have made. In those days there was no tradition among anthropologists of belaboring what was to them obvious: if you wanted to learn about the way of life of some group of people, you went to live among them to whatever extent was appropriate and possible. Educational researchers, with their heavy borrowing of measurement techniques and experimental design from psychology, recognized no "method" at all in the approach of the field ethnographer.

In that climate we hardly imagined "anthropology and education" would gain recognition in either its discipline of orientation or its arena of practice. Who would have guessed that ethnographic research (which increasingly came to be called ethnographic "method" once educators started talking about it) would be so central in the influence of anthropology upon educational researchers? Careful explication of my study as method would have been timely and might help to account for the book's popularity, *if* I had anticipated that potential interest in the ethnographic approach.

A second source of bafflement is that although the book admirably catalogs problems, it offers little in the way of solutions. Even at that, the book goes farther than I originally intended. The six pages comprising the final chapter, "In Retrospect and Prospect," were added at the insistence of publisher's reviewers who felt that readers would expect more and that, with three years for further reflection, there must be more I could say about educating minority group children. Those three years have now lengthened to 25, and once again I am struggling to identify whatever insight I have achieved that might prove helpful, but neither have the problems receded into the past nor the solutions become more apparent.

I have written only one other article directly concerned with the Kwakiutl experience. It was titled "The Teacher as an Enemy," first appearing in George Spindler's 1974 collection *Education and Cultural Process* and now available in a revised second edition published in 1987 by Waveland Press. In that article I invite teachers to consider other perspectives for viewing the teacher-student relationship in addition to the one that probably characterizes their own personal experience, that of teacher as friend and helper.

As my comments no doubt reveal, even today I will be satisfied if I am able to offer provocative and constructive ways to think about the *problems*. At the time I was writing, I felt a responsibility to present the case without yielding to the urge to offer facile solutions or to suggest that there were "answers" if we could just find them. I seriously doubted, however, that a book laden with problems-without-solutions would find an audience among educators already aware of what is wrong and frustrated in their call for help with what to do about it. However, some teacher readers have mentioned how refreshing it is to find an author grappling with problems in his own classroom rather than indicting them for problems assumed to exist in theirs.

Admittedly, I do not know who the book's readers have been; perhaps I am correct in my suspicions that its audience included few experienced teachers. But somewhere — perhaps in teacher preparation programs addressing issues of multi-cultural education — one must account for thousands of readers (those 20,000 copies sold and often resold; library copies read and re-read) who should have recognized — at the conclusion of their reading, if not at the beginning — that in their chosen profession, problems related to the social context of schooling far outstrip the magnitude of our understanding.

Another source of bafflement was my feeling that the negative cast of the account would turn readers off — and possibly turn them away — rather than engage them with the complexity of the issue. I have never spent another year, before or since, as intense as my year at Blackfish Village. I felt an obligation to portray that experience candidly, rather than to whitewash it or to hide behind a facade of scientific objectivity. My strong and positive feelings toward many of the people individually were offset by an uneasiness while living at the village that was nurtured by acts and accusations of petty and sometimes not-so-petty theft, petty and sometimes not-so-petty violence and crime.

An official of the Indian Affairs Branch, in those days the unit that staffed and operated Canada's Indian schools, reacted strongly to the newly published monograph, admonishing me for preparing so negative an account. "How will we ever recruit teachers for these schools once they read a book like yours?" he queried. I was so taken aback that I do not recall offering a reply, but since that moment I have frequently quoted him to make a counterpoint: in terms of teacher recruitment alone, my efforts seem worthwhile if I headed off even one or two of the disastrous placements that continue to occur in comparable outpost schools in parts of Alaska and Canada (to name two places within my own experience). Teachers who seek and accept such assignments are often totally unprepared for the potential physical *and social* duress of rural living under extreme environmental conditions, compounded by difficulties of cross-cultural misunderstanding and the inevitability of village factionalism. Happily, the reaction of that one official was not the majority reaction.

My portrayal of village life was intended to be neither complimentary nor defamatory. I invoked Walt Whitman's words to underscore that intent. I sought to be objective but discrete. In the interest of the latter, my discretion necessarily goes unremarked, while questions of possible indiscretion may arise for each reader anew.

My choice of whether and how to report the vocabulary of certain villagers, particularly after drinking parties, was critical. I decided to quote speech as I heard it, in a day when vernacular language was treated daintily, especially in texts or scholarly works. (To illustrate: In the original galley proofs sent to me, all expletives had been deleted, the result of overzealous copyediting that replaced them with equally telltale dashes. The margins of the author's proofs that I returned made for rather startling reading in themselves!) In turn, language reported in the book distressed some of my most valued Kwakiutl friends, giving me second thoughts long after the deed was done.

On the other hand, the straightforwardness of the account proved to be one of its strengths. Even my directness with language drew unexpected support from Reggie's grandfather, the one individual whose judgement of the completed work was most critical to me personally. Discussing the book shortly after its publication, another prominent elder expressed dismay to Reggie's grandfather at the "poor image" created of Kwakiutl people, noting particular concern for the drunken comportment and "bad language" I had so meticulously chronicled. " 'But Jimmy,' I said to him," the Old Man related when next we met, " 'you know that Harry's book tells about the village just the way it is.' "

Were I to initiate the study today, pursuing the same problem orientation — to investigate why Indian pupils so often fail in school — most likely I would follow a similar course in conducting the research. Accepting a position as classroom teacher — a role in which I was both qualified and experienced — gave me a legitimate status in the village and was virtually the only full-time role available to an outsider. Although the children represented much of what was lively about the village, I chafed at being isolated day after day with them in the schoolhouse, thereby having to miss aspects of everyday village life. Only later did I realize that I might (and should) have attended *more* rather than less to these young Kwakiutl, as I will discuss below.

With my overriding concern for education, I would again give particular attention to schooling, although in organizing the presentation I would begin with a description of the community before introducing the topic of formal education, just as I did earlier. At Blackfish Village, differences in the cultural systems underlying community and school were nicely accommodated by presenting the account in two major sections.

Nevertheless, I would make several changes if I were repeating the study. First, I would make more extensive use of case studies of individual children, focusing the village and classroom accounts even more closely on the same five (or perhaps only one or two) school-age children. In part that reflects my growing interest in life history approaches in ethnography as well as in drawing upon anthropology to expand the scope of our inquiries in education. I draw a general maxim from Alfred North Whitehead, who suggests that we should do less more thoroughly, and an anthropological one from Clifford Geertz, who cautions that there is no ascent to truth without a corresponding descent to cases.

I did not approach the original fieldwork with studies of individual children in mind. Working in so small a village, efforts to preserve anonymity might make such focused study impractical, but in rethinking how to conduct and present the fieldwork I certainly would explore the possibility. For example, I might have made Reggie's story central to the school, perhaps contrasting it with his grandfather's story in portraying the village. The Old Man made it clear that he would have enjoyed a more central role in my account (or in a sequel in which he recounted his life story to me), similar to the role he played in my well-being at the village and my eventually achieving new insight about humans in general and the integrity of "being Indian" in particular.

Another stylistic change would be to write almost entirely in the past tense rather than employ the "ethnographic present" still popular among anthropologists. True, the past tense seems to "kill off" everybody as soon as an action is completed, but present quickly becomes past, and I wish I had not left my pupils in eternal youth, trudging up the path to a school that no longer exists in a village that has been totally deserted for 20 years.

There are other changes, also editorial, that have come with the times. Students in my classes today are quick (and correct) to point out that my preoccupation with the preferred usage of "that" and "which" must have begun *after* I wrote this study. On the other hand, it was correct in those days to use the masculine pronoun for indefinite references to people, and preferable to write in the singlar to avoid ambiguities of "they" and "their." Today it is not correct. Even language does not remain the same! Indeed, if a small but vocal group, particularly individuals active in the U'mista Cultural Society centered at Alert Bay, can exert enough influence, the term Kwakiutl itself that anthropologists assigned long ago, as well as the parallel term Kwawkewlth used by government agencies, may give way to Kwakwaka'wakw, a term referring to all Kwak'wala speakers rather than only to one village group (Fort Rupert, the Kwagu'l) where it was spoken.

RECONCEPTUALIZING THE STUDY

I cannot imagine, however, that I would take the same problem orientation. My approach to the fieldwork would be similar and, had I not aged by these same

25 years, I would *probably* be willing to assume again the dual (and in some ways antithetical) roles of teacher and anthropologist. But in the intervening years, "anthropology and education" has taken form and substance as an interdisciplinary inquiry and I have found a niche for myself as a shaper of that form and a contributor to that substance. Following the direction set by George Spindler, my mentor and colleague of almost 3 decades, today I would give far more attention to cultural transmission. Even more specifically, my efforts would focus on *cultural acquisition:* how each child acquires his or her particular version of what the world is about.

In that earlier day, the educator part of me was totally preoccupied with what my pupils did *not* know. Like village teachers before and since, I found the pupils "behind" and saw a mandate in trying to get them "caught up." Today, the anthropologist part of me would pose the problem differently: granted these pupils do not know many (most?) of the things I, as teacher, want them to know (e.g., to speak standard English, to be able to "read, write, and do arithmetic"), what is it that they *do* know? If they are inattentive to what is accepted as important in *my* world, then to what do they attend in theirs?

What, for example, is the underlying structure of language as each of them individually has worked it out? Just think what an incredible laboratory I had: a multilingual classroom where some children heard only Kwakwala at home, most heard a mixture of Kwakwala and English, a few heard essentially English (because their parents had made a conscious linguistic choice for the presumed benefit of their children, or because English was the language the parents themselves had in common). How and when do children code-switch to accommodate multiple dialects and different listeners? I have heard experienced teachers in similar village settings argue that their pupils, caught between dying native languages and nonstandard English, have "no language at all." Linguists insist this cannot be the case; teachers insist that it is. A linguist would have had a field day in my Kwakiutl classroom. With how much training might I have been a more linguistically-sensitive observer?

Conversely, might even a bit more thinking about language acquisition, and efforts and accomplishments in studying it, have provided an analog for looking at cultural acquisition? Even preschool village children made distinctions between things Indian and things white. Where did they draw the line between these two cultural influences? What does a contemporary 6-year-old or 16-year-old Kwakiutl know? They were all in my classroom — hour upon hour every day — yet how little I learned of what *they* knew in my penchant to get them to learn more of what I knew. How I discounted the value of their knowledge and inflated the worth of my own.

Cultural acquisition would be my focus today: an anthropological inquiry into what children *do* know, rather than an educator preoccupation with what they *do not* know.

At first blush, it might seem the teacher role would not be well served by that orientation. Teachers, after all, should be teaching their pupils, not learning from them! Or should they? What might result if learners felt that their own knowledge was valued, their interests deemed interesting, their ability to survive day-to-day under possibly adverse conditions respected, their ways of figuring things out regarded as reasonable, even if they might lack the elegance of the teacher's practiced solutions? What might happen in a classroom that celebrated how much its participants knew rather than doted only on their deficiencies? Or a classroom that helped individuals look introspectively into their lives to discover how and why some things they "know" vary from the versions that others, including neighbors and even siblings with seemingly identical backgrounds, carry about in their heads?

This focus on cultural acquisition might seem to imply particular interest on my part in two topics: how children sort between elements of white culture and elements of Indian culture, and a preoccupation with "things learned at school." Although those topics are of more than passing interest, neither seems an appropriate starting (or ending) place for the line of inquiry I am proposing. Let me explain.

My anthropologist colleague Malcolm McFee cautioned years ago that if there was going to be an anthropology of education, there should be something distinctly anthropological about it. By commitment and training, educators have their work cut out for them in defining what it is that teachers should be trying to put into the heads of students and assessing the extent to which it actually gets there. The anthropological complement to that well-intended effort might be to help teachers understand and appreciate what is *already* in the heads of their students, the existing mass to which new knowledge must be linked if it is to become personal knowledge. School learning is of interest to the anthropologist's concern for cultural acquisition only as an aspect of a far more comprehensive question: What is it that any particular child, of a particular age and as a member of a particular social group, knows?

As to sorting ideas and behaviors into two distinct and mutually exclusive categories, things "Indian" and things "white," it strikes me as more important for the anthropological observer to try to discern *whether* and *how* individuals at different ages accomplish any such sorting than to assume that macrocultural distinctions so axiomatic to government officials, educators, and even anthropologists, are necessarily even recognized. Imposing rigid Indian-culture, white-culture taxonomies leads to drawing a conclusion similar to the one teachers in cross-cultural settings sometimes draw about student proficiency in the prevailing languages: that their students are deficient in both. With old Indian ways dying out and new white ways inadequately learned, villagers are denied "culture" on the same basis they are denied language. The terms "linguistic deprivation" and "cultural deprivation" were frequently employed in the 1960s to explain school failure.

I should not be one to scoff at such explanations: I came perilously close to laying part of the blame for the failure of Indian pupils on "linguistic deprivation" (p. 129). Fortunately, I qualified my observation by locating it in terms of one setting where it does hold, "for the purposes of the school." What I might have done as teacher, given a realistic appraisal of the language facility and language needs of my pupils (at least for successful interaction in mainstream Canadian society), would have been to encourage classroom conversation and to see whether I could gradually increase the ratio of English. But anyone who has managed a classroom of as many as 29 elementary school children (not to mention a one-room school with a ten year age span) probably can guess that my class was organized toward exactly the opposite goal: obedient silence. Indeed, as the year progressed, there was less and less classroom talk, even on my part.

In spite of the fact that I recognized the phrase itself as "inadequate and misleading," I was more vulnerable to "cultural deprivation" explanations of school failure. I yielded to a way of thinking about culture strongly influenced by the origins of the term as a social science concept, comparable to contemporary ways of thinking about human intelligence — that there is one optimal form of it and that not everyone enjoys the full measure achieved by those preoccupied with assessing it. Transitional ("marginal" was another popular term then) peoples like those of Blackfish Village were viewed as having lost most of the elements of their former culture without having replaced them with comparable elements from the newly dominant one. I leaned on explanations that saw villagers exhibiting a "truncated" or "partial" culture in my effort to account for what I perceived as cultural inadequacy, although I resisted the idea that they were "cultureless."

What I now take to be a more instructive way of viewing culture has been suggested by anthropologist Ward Goodenough in a paper first published in 1976 (in the forerunner of today's *Anthropology and Education Quarterly*) entitled "Multiculturalism as the Normal Human Experience." Goodenough urges us to regard human beings individually as the locus of what *collectively* can be regarded as the "culture" of some interacting group of humans, when standards of behavior are held sufficiently in common by its members to allow satisfactory social intercourse. Goodenough has proposed the term "propriospect" to label this "private, subjective view of the world and its contents" that each of us acquires out of the totality of our personal experience (see his *Culture, Language, and Society,* Benjamin/Cummings, 1981, p. 98 ff.).

No functioning human ever lacks a propriospect or has only a partial, or truncated, or "inadequate" one. Each human has a unique propriospect. Every human's propriospect includes versions of appropriate roles within at least one macrocultural system, together with a version of all the particular roles in all the attendant microcultural systems in which he or she is expected to exhibit competence.

The propriospect of each village child included, therefore, his or her age-and-gender-specific working conception of western Canadian mainstream culture, in a coastal logging-and-fishing-community form appropriate for the Alert Bay region of the early 1960s. To some extent each child's propriospect had been modified by intentionally educative influences (like the school or Indian Health Service or missionaries of the day) as well as a constant barrage of casual influences ranging from visitors and visits, cinema and radio, reading, and the sporadic but critical interaction of family members and themselves with a host of seen and unseen agents that virtually controlled their social and economic lives as Canadian citizens.

Their propriospects also included their age-and-gender-specific working conceptions of Canadian Indian culture, in a 1960s, Kwakwala-speaking, Blackfish Village variety. Each child's propriospect also had been modified by intentionally educative influences (like important potlatches or inter-village sports and social events) and a constant barrage of casual influences, particularly with visits and visitors that provided opportunity to experience, both firsthand and through the accounts of others, a sense of (a sometimes cohesive) Indian community among neighboring villages, among Kwakwala-speaking people of the region, and a pan-Indianism that allied them with other unseen agents of their own on both sides of the Canadian border.

As village teacher, I nicely illustrated Goodenough's point that every human acquires competence in at least *one* macro- or national cultural system: my competence was in (and remains limited essentially to) mainstream North American culture, particularly its male, white, middle-class, English-speaking, West Coast variety. My teacher role neither required nor assumed competence in Kwakiutl culture. Had it not been for anthropological interests, I would not necessarily have known anything about the Kwakiutl or about North American Indians at all: such knowledge was not part of the job description. The only important question was whether I knew how to ''run'' a school, a competence acquired in *my* cultural system, not in that of the villagers.

Reggie's grandfather, on the other hand, illustrates Goodenough's complementary point: humans often acquire competence in two or more macrocultural systems. Born and raised in an earlier day when Indian and white differences in western Canada were more readily distinguishable, the Old Man had acquired competence in two recognizably different cultural systems. He could ''talk Indian,'' had experienced many of the old ways of his people firsthand, and could manipulate (and be manipulated) within Kwakiutl social systems of family, *numima,* community, and ''people.'' But he could also speak, read, and write English, had acquired many of the ''new ways'' of mainstream western North America (his was the family with the highest average grade-level attainment in school, his the village home with two-way radio communication to Alert Bay, his among the seine boats with the latest technological equipment) and he could manipulate (and be manipulated) within mainstream Canadian social and economic systems that included government benefits and regulations, commercial business negotiations, seine boat skippers and their fish packing companies, and the Anglican church.

Anthropologist Goodenough reminds us that even for those of us whose competence is limited essentially to one macroculture — as in my own case — we are *all* multicultural. All humans acquire competence in myriad microcultures and their subcultural variants within at least one macrocultural system. At the same time, we do not need to acquire complete mastery of other social systems in order to interact with individuals in them. I did not have to be competent in Kwakiutl culture to be able to manage a one-room school in a rural Canadian community. It did not even matter that I was American rather than Canadian: at least I said ''with'' rather than ''mit,'' and I could hum ''God Save the Queen'' even if I didn't have the words quite right at first.

Similarly, Reggie's grandfather did not need competence in all the nuances of social interaction for individuals from all the various social systems with whom he came into occasional contact: Chinese shopkeepers of Alert Bay, Finnish settlers of nearby Sointula, crews of the ''Yugoslav'' fishing boats, Indian people from different Northwest Coast groups. As they did with their verbal discourse, members of these diverse groups could switch to their common orientation in mainstream western Canadian *culture* to conduct their mutual affairs. For all the diversity of their individual propriospects, there was sufficient recognition of and competence in a National Culture that they could interact, intermarry, and even (rather begrudgingly, it often seems to outsiders) admit to some common purposes and identity in being Canadian.

Today, Reggie has acquired and continues to acquire the competence *he* needs in conducting his life. He moves even more easily than his grandfather did among and between Indian and non-Indian associates. But he does not have to surrender a measure of ''Indian'' competence for each measure of non-Indian competence he acquires: cultural competencies are not mutually exclusive, to be acquired as if in a zero-sum game where each competence gained necessitates a corresponding competence lost.

I assume that Reggie will continue to add to his repertory of cultural competencies both in Indian *and* non-Indian ways — as he had learned to do even before I first met him as a six-year-old — to seek self-consciously to have and to be ''the best'' in both societies. That is how he was raised by parents and grandparents whose ambitions for themselves are now vested in him. Because he sets his marks so high, personal ambition itself may prove his undoing. On the other hand, maybe he is one of those individuals who sees himself poised rather than caught between two cultures, inclined to see opportunity where many find only cause for despair. If such individuals are relatively rare, at least they are not a romantic fiction. I have known them personally among the Kwakiutl, and they did not all ''die out'' with Reggie's grandfather's generation. It's simply easier to acknowledge those who succeeded during bygone eras than to recognize with certainty their counterparts in the process of trying to make it today.

TEACHING ACROSS CULTURES

Formal education is predicated on the notion of learner incompetence. Education across cultures exacerbates the magnitude of that incompetence by identifying worthy knowledge as something located entirely outside the cultural system of the student. We continue to perceive multicultural education as a problem of the student, a problem to which teachers and schools supposedly are the answer. We are correct with this approach often enough. Education frequently ''takes,'' and we witness wave upon wave of refugee and immigrant and minority groups successfully incorporated into new communities and nations.

But sometimes the lines are drawn differently, especially in cases where indigenous minorities see themselves as overrun, dislocated, or threatened with involuntary assimilation. In such settings, resistance to ''the system,'' or to the teacher as its spokesperson, may become an entrenched student strategy, a posture readily adopted as appropriate behavior within one's group even though the underlying basis for antagonism is not well understood, especially among its youngest antagonists. Such was the case at Blackfish Village.

I did not set out to find the roots of that antagonism or attempt to eradicate it. I do not recommend that teachers individually adopt such goals as their professional mission or personal crusade. I did not create the tensions between white and Indian groups, nor did I see as my role the responsibility to singlehandedly resolve them. I could not help wishing I could make things ''better,'' although I felt a clearer (and more realistic) sense of purpose in trying to keep them from becoming worse. But what about considering that different perspective suggested in the closing sentences of the original monograph, looking at the school as the problem and pondering whether in any way students might be viewed as the answer?

Were I faced today with the Kwakiutl classroom that I met in 1962, as both teacher and researcher I would attempt to approach the setting differently. I would devote my major *intellectual* effort to trying to discern what the children already knew and knew about (individually, collectively) and how they had gone about acquiring that knowledge, even if my major *physical* effort went to "running" the school. My strategy would be to learn from and about my students and, in the process, to try to make them self-conscious "knowers" about the processes of knowing. By no means would this be as easy as it may sound: my interest in virtually anything to do with the lives of village pupils usually had the effect of causing them to "clam up," perhaps preceded by a hostilely delivered, "What do *you* want to know for?" They did show interest in aspects of my personal life, however, particularly in my family upbringing and childhood experiences — me as person, rather than me as teacher. Swapping stories, comparing settings, looking for universals, might be the way to get a dialogue going.

In time, I think even recalcitrant pupils *might* be encouraged to share glimpses into their world as they have come to understand it. That understanding — *their* understanding — of the universe would provide my orienting focus. One might begin by inventorying the skills and recipes young people have for doing things and making choices, discerning the maps in their heads that provide routes connecting persons and places in their known world. Eventually we might be able to examine their ways of sorting and categorizing elements identified in that world and some attendant attitudes and beliefs. And that might open the way for inquiry into how and why other people in other places organize and categorize their "worlds," on similar or different bases. The approach seems worth a try in a classroom where nothing else appears to be working. I am not the only teacher to observe the difference between silent, sullen Indian children in the classroom and talkative, even bossy ones outside it.

I would not abdicate my role as teacher, but I would soften its pedantic aspects and strengthen its inquiring ones. On reflection, my rigid curricular preoccupation of those days seems a bit misguided. Such rigor might have been tempered had the thought crossed my mind that I would outlive the majority of my young pupils. Although it flies quite in the face of the back-to-basics educational mood of the 1980s, I continue to wonder if I might have identified, or created, more teachable moments through an "inquiring" approach than a formal, traditional scope and sequence ever can generate.

Through three decades of teaching I have become less and less concerned or content with merely doling out knowledge. That is not to say that I object to curriculum efforts at scope and sequence; my very use of the phrase "teachable moments" implies that there are things I expect to teach and that I have some sense of what I might want 12- or 20-year-old students to learn beyond what I would want 8-year-olds to learn. The scope and sequence of North American schools, incredibly uniform as it is, might be viewed as a common "experience" to which all children are subjected — perhaps with a bit more abandon than we customarily see in schools, but a shared experience, nonetheless.

I have never been one to insist that schooling must be relevant. School experience is probably at its best — and maybe is most effective as well — when it is wildly irrelevant, particularly in terms of the classroom's own well-ordered routines. Given the years and years we devote to "schooling" our youth, the skills-and-training aspects can be tightly packaged and efficiently taught with plenty of time left for wonderment, even in the least permissive of educational climates. We can all speed up the lesson when we have to. Cultural repertories consist of far more than techniques and recipes.

The important difference, however, would not be in teaching style but in teacher stance — to recognize every pupil as a profound knower-and-wonderer-about-certain-things (but not about everything, and not necessarily what I wonder about). As both researcher and teacher, I would dwell more on the already known of their way of life rather than be preoccupied solely with what they did not know of mine. Before we try as educators to "catch people up," we need to have a better idea of the anthropologist's concern for where they already have been and what they already understand that enables them to cope, just as we do, one day at a time. And then educator and parent, and maybe even anthropologist, can attempt to address the difficult issues of where they are headed, what they seek for the next generation, the social costs and risks that may be involved, and the extent to which the school *possibly* may be of help.

POSTSCRIPT

In the interim between first drafting these words and mailing a final version to the publisher many months later, I received the sad news that Reggie, at age 31, had taken his own life, apparently despondent over a pending separation and the thought of losing custody of his beloved children. Only ten days earlier we had the opportunity of a good visit, made possible by an extended closure during the 1986 fall fishing season reminiscent of the problems about which fishermen were complaining 25 years ago. Although Reggie remained unimpressed with the book ("It's so out-of-date"), his reaction to the new Waveland edition was, "That should have been me on the cover."

I had intended originally to conclude this Afterword by honoring the memory of Reggie's grandfather, *Kla-kli-li-tla,* not only for the full and rich four score years of his life but in recognition of the influence he continues to exert even today through words and deeds well remembered and carefully recounted. As a younger member of the family reflected, "No one thought I paid any attention. But everything he said, I can still hear now, and I listen to him."

Without that same sense of celebration, I mark Reggie's tragic death as well, a young life still in the making. But during that recent visit to Kwakiutl country I heard and saw evidence of other young adults assuming responsibility for maintaining links with the past and making appropriate adaptations for the present, and of mature adults assuming the mantle of elder to offer guidance and encouragement.

Reggie's concern was that Indian ways are dying out. Watching today as Kwakiutl pupils bring home computerized report cards or navigate local shopping malls can buttress that impression. Still, my sense is that although personal circumstances may alter dramatically, the underlying interpersonal rhythms and patterned ways of coping that I attribute to "being Kwakiutl" seem to endure. Indian *people* do the dying; figuratively, so can entire villages. Yet Indian *ways* are faring pretty well. Kwakiutl culture most certainly has changed through time, not only in the 100 years since Franz Boas began systematically to describe it, but even in the quarter century of my own firsthand experience. As long traditions must, however, it is also proving remarkably resilient.

H.F.W.

Eugene, Oregon